GRACE HELPS

A W.O.R.T.H.Y. STUDY

Romans 5-8

Beth Steffaniak

To my beautiful and sweet grandsons, Samson and Ezra. My prayer is that you would grow to love God's word and allow the gospel to transform your lives. Even though you are still very young—too young to even read—maybe this book can be just one resource among many that points you in the direction of God one day.

Table of Contents

Worthy Method v

Introduction to Romans 5-8 ix

Week One xi

1 – Reasons to Rejoice 13

2 – A Love that Compels 17

3 – The Many Sides of God's Love 21

Week Two 25

4 – From Man to Son of Man 27

5 – What's Lost and Gained 31

6 – God's Grace is Greater 35

Week Three 39

7 – Grace Taken for Granted? 41

8 – United in Death and Life 45

9 – Slain and Set Free 49

Week Four 53

10 – Emancipation Proclamation 55

11 – 'Altar' Your Life 59

12 – Fork in the Road 63

Week Five 67

13 – Free Hearts 69

14 – Good Fruit 73

15 – The Christ-follower's Comma 77

Week Six 81

16 – Who are You Devoted to? 83

17 – New Source and Way 87

18 – X-Ray Vision 91

Week Seven 95

19 – The 'Silent Killer' 97

20 – The Christian's Conundrum 101

21 – The 'Intruder' Within 105

Week Eight 109

22 – Dreadful Versus Delightful 111

23 – Death Defying 115

24 – Right and Might 119

Week Nine 123

25 – Set on Life or Death? 125

26 – Signs of Life... 129

27 – Empty Hands 133

Week Ten 137

28 – Who's Your Daddy? 139

29 – Leaning into Christ's Glory 143

30 – Worth All the Pain 147

Week Eleven 151

31 – Wait Patiently 153

32 – Known, Honed and Blessed.................................... 157

33 – Always For—Never Against................................... 161

Week Twelve 165

34 – Christ Rests His Case 167

35 – God's Love Conquers All 171

36 – Sure of His Love...175

Worthy Method

And so, from the day we heard, we have not ceased to pray for you, asking that you may be filled with the knowledge of his will in all spiritual wisdom and understanding, so as to walk in a manner worthy of the Lord, fully pleasing to him: bearing fruit in every good work and increasing in the knowledge of God (Colossians 1:9-10 ESV).

Although the Apostle Paul prayed this prayer thousands of years ago, I'm praying this prayer for you too, my friend!

Isn't that such a great and noble calling? To walk in a manner worthy of the Lord, bearing spiritual fruit for Him out of our growing knowledge of God and His word? That is what I long to do and is also one of the reasons I love the WORTHY method of Bible study since the acrostic reminds me daily of this calling and Christ-honoring pursuit.

Before we look at the nuts and bolts of the WORTHY method, I'd like to give you some guidance on how to approach the study. One of the best ways to read and use this book is to purchase my WORTHY Journal, available on Amazon. However, buying a blank notebook to write out your study notes can be just as useful and will certainly save you a bit of cash. If you're a computer geek like me, you might prefer to keep a running document on your computer instead of writing out your notes by hand. Whichever way you go, your written notes will motivate you to stick with your studies, giving you a sense of investment and ownership in this noble process of understanding and applying God's word better. Not only that but you'll give yourself tangible reminders of what God is teaching you all along the way.

If your schedule is crammed and spare time is scarce, you could forgo writing your notes in a journal and simply read this book as a brief three-days-a-week devotional, with both the Scriptures for the day and my study notes included for reflection. Although this is certainly a helpful and encouraging way to gain something from your daily readings, I'd discourage you from relying on my notes every day. Only take this route when your schedule is too packed to do the study for yourself. Then challenge yourself all along the way to carve out the time to write out and do your own studies in addition to reading the book.

If you find yourself becoming dependent on my notes, be sure to hold off reviewing them each day until you start gaining the habit of writing out your own notes. Don't miss out on the blessings that God offers those who do as 2 Timothy 2:15 describes, "Do your best to present yourself to God as one approved, a worker who has no need to be ashamed, rightly handling the word of truth."

I've used and referred to the English Standard Version (ESV) for my studies in this Grace Helps Bible study. I chose the ESV because it is considered one of the most accurate word-for-word translations of the Bible. But feel free to use your favorite version or, even better, compare your version with others like ESV, including those in a parallel Bible to gain a broader view between versions.

Before diving into each day's study, it's always best to familiarize yourself with the context of Romans (or whatever book of the Bible you might be studying). I've provided some of my own research on the entire book of Romans in the first of this series, Grace Covers (Romans 1-4), and have also included a snapshot of the context and themes for chapters 5 through 8 in this book. But I would encourage you to do some additional research on your own, investigating the context and current events that occurred during and leading up to the writing of Romans. I promise you'll gain a sense of adventure and wonder as you dig into the historical setting and customs. It will help bring it alive for you.

Before you begin this study, you might want to read the entire Romans chapters 5-8 to gain a birds-eye view of Paul's letter. Let the words leap off the page and into your heart, not stopping at various points to dissect and examine their meaning just yet. Each time you come to a new chapter in your studies, reread it before you begin the study of that particular day's Scripture.

I find it very helpful to refer to various commentaries that I trust, taking in what they say about each passage I might be studying. I encourage you to do that also. I trust and utilize several online and free commentary sites, such as enduringword.com, studylight.org, preceptaustin.org, and biblehub.com, referring to gotquestions.org and desiring.org on occasion as well.

Just a word of warning. Do not depend on these scholars to do the interpreting for you. Instead, use them as guides and guardians that help keep you on track. Anytime you hit something that continues to be confusing or seems controversial, seek the Lord's illumination, going further to prooftext your studies with the help of wise spiritual leaders in your church and life.

Once you've completed these initial steps, you're ready to dive into Grace Helps using the WORTHY Bible study method. This method provides various prompts for writing out your own insights, formulating an application, chronicling your prayer based on what you've studied, challenging you to a yielded response that you apply with your "Thought to take" all day long.

After you've completed your studies, I hope you'll refer to my daily notes as an added point of view. My notes can also serve as a model for how to research and pray the scriptures you've studied. If you wait to refer to my notes until after you've done your own work, you'll likely discover something you didn't notice or know about the text. Even better, *you* might discover something that I didn't see or identify. When that happens, we will be putting Hebrew 4:24 into practice— "spurring one another on to love and good works." Ready to head out on this journey? Take my hand, and let's go together!

W.O.R.T.H.Y. Method

Welcome the Lord: Welcome God to reveal His truth to you as you study.

Open my eyes, that I may behold wondrous things out of your law.
—Psalm 119:18

Observe what Scripture says:

Read the Scripture passage aloud once, though twice is even better. Then use your favorite version to write out word-for-word what you observe each verse says in your Bible study journal. Do not forgo this step! It really hones your observation skills and helps you better retain what you just studied in Scripture. These practices and advantages will give you insights into the biblical gems hidden in plain sight.

Recognize what is noteworthy and true:

Recognize and research the context of each passage. Find out who wrote it and what was going on in the author's (or his audience's) life at the time of the writing. Then record all the details that you recognize one-by-one, word-for-word.

Notice the important truths to know and follow, sins to avoid, including what is inspiring, repeated, odd, alludes to Christ, reveals God's nature, etc. Make identifying biblical truths—distinguishing them from the lies you might be embracing—one of your primary goals as you write out your notes in your journal.

Thought to take:

Look over the truths you have gleaned and write out what thought you want to take with you throughout your day. Doing this helps you integrate God's word into your life, enabling you to live in a manner worthy of the Lord. Then summarize and write down the thought(s) into a concise action step under "T2t." Keep this thought and challenge in a visible spot so you'll be reminded at random points to apply it during your day. Without this additional step, you're likely to forget and miss opportunities to live out God's word in your day.

Help from the Lord:

Write out a prayer loosely based on the passage for the day similar to how I have prayed under each "Help" prompt. Doing this involves expressing your desire for God's help as well as committing to obey the biblical truths related to that day's reading.

You might also want to pray the Scripture more directly, using the passage for the day as a template for your prayer. Simply personalize the verses, praying from your heart, while staying close to the verbiage found in the text.

Then as you go about your day, whisper a prayer related to your T2t in both moments of joy and difficulty.

Yield to the Lord:

When you feel you are at a crossroads in your day, being tempted or simply feel weak, remind yourself of you focus and thought for the day so you can surrender your desires and choose God's will and way instead.

Consider also reflecting on this prompt and challenge at the end of your day, identifying both the times you yielded and times you resisted. Ask the Lord to give you greater insight into how to stand on His truth and yield your way for His as you move forward each day.

Introduction to Romans 5-8

What was going on historically during the time this letter was written?

The Apostle Paul wrote Romans approximately 56-58 AD when the Roman Empire was under the rule of a young 16-year-old Emperor Nero. However, it wasn't until sometime around 64 AD that Nero began fiercely persecuting the church and slaughtering Christ-followers. The believers in the church of Rome likely felt the tides turning against them even in the earlier days before the persecution of Christians ran rampant. Whether they knew about the persecution to come or not, God knew and was preparing them through Paul's ministry and this letter to the Roman church and beyond.

Overarching Theme

Sanctification by faith in Christ.

"Sanctification" is the Spirit's helpful work within the believer, setting Christ-followers apart and making them holy for God's purposes and plan. It is the spiritual growth process every true believer must experience, persevere in, and display to the world. The more God helps sanctify a believer through His grace, the more the believer looks like Christ.

Themes by Chapter

Chapter 5: Reconciled—no longer condemned.

Chapter 6: Resurrected—dead to sin, alive to God.

Chapter 7: Released—freed from the tyranny of the law.

Chapter 8: Represented—adopted, helped, and loved.

What specific issues did Paul address in chapter 5?

The benefits of justification through Christ (vv. 1-11).

The reasons for justification (vv. 12-14).

How justification was paid for and given to believers (vv. 15-21).

What specific issues did Paul address in chapter 6?

Dying to sinful living, enabling believers to live in unity with Christ (vv. 1-14).

Becoming a slave of Christ through the process of "sanctification"—the working out of your salvation (vv. 15-23).

What specific issues did Paul address in chapter 7?

The role and arousal of the law in our hearts (vv. 1-12).

The spiritual war ignited by our sin nature (vv. 13-25).

What specific issues did Paul address in chapter 8?

Christ set us free from the death sentence required by the law (vv. 1-4).

How to set our minds on the things of the Spirit (vv. 5-13).

Recognizing our adoption as children of God (vv. 14-17).

Suffering and how to wait well on the Lord (vv. 18-25).

The Spirit's help and intercession in our suffering (vv. 26-28).

God's predetermined choice of His own (vv. 29-30).

God's extravagant love and help in all of life's troubles (vv. 31-39).

Week One

1 – Reasons to Rejoice

Week 1, Day 1—Romans 5:1-4

Welcome the Lord!

Open my eyes, that I may behold wondrous things out of your law.
—Psalm 119:18

Observe what the Scripture says:

1 – Therefore, since we have been justified by faith, we have peace with God through our Lord Jesus Christ.
2 – Through him we have also obtained access by faith into this grace in which we stand, and we rejoice in hope of the glory of God.
3 – Not only that, but we rejoice in our sufferings, knowing that suffering produces endurance,
4 – and endurance produces character, and character produces hope,

Recognize what is noteworthy and true:

This chapter ushers in something of a shift in focus for Paul's teaching thus far in Romans. Before this, he had fully stated the case for how God justifies those who believe in Christ rather than relying on the law for salvation. But here in chapter 5, he moved toward explaining the many benefits of justification, with verse 1 reestablishing this starting point: **"Therefore, since we have been justified by faith, we have peace with God through our Lord Jesus Christ."** Since Paul used past tense here for "justified," we are reminded that God does not need to continually justify believers. Justification is done and completed when God counts a believer's faith as righteousness just like God counted Abraham's faith as righteousness (Romans 4:9). God views the believer as innocent because Christ's innocence and sacrifice cover each believer's sin. Peace with God is an incredible benefit and is different from the peace of God. Peace "with" God means that God no longer considers a believer to be His enemy. But once God justifies the believer, he or she is free to continually experience the peace of God, which provides serenity and calmness through our dependence on Him.

In verse 2, Paul revealed yet another benefit of the believer's justification, **"Through him we have also obtained access by faith into this grace in which we stand, and we rejoice in hope of the glory of God."** A believer's faith also grants him or her the benefit of access to God's grace. The verb tense of "access" in Greek clarifies that this is a permanent possession for believers. God first extends grace—His unmerited favor and forgiveness—to those who place their faith in Christ. Then He continually extends grace to believers, helping us to stand in His grace no matter what comes against us. The Christ-follower may fall down due to sin but never falls away from God. Our Father's grace is always there to pick us up and establish our feet again on the firm foundation of Christ. All of this gives us reason to "rejoice"—better translated, "boast"—in the hope of the glory of God. If we try to justify ourselves through good works, we steal glory from God. But when we keep our hope in Christ alone, all of God's glory flows perfectly to Him and His throne!

Paul listed even more benefits of justification, adding, **"Not only that, but we rejoice in our sufferings, knowing that suffering produces endurance, and endurance produces character, and character produces hope,"** (vv. 3 and 4). The Greek word used for "sufferings" here is "tribulum" and is where the English word for "tribulations" is derived. In Paul's day, a tribulum was a heavy, spike-covered piece of timber that was pulled over grain to separate and refine the wheat from the useless chaff. Suffering works in the same way. It gives us the ability to endure under the harshest of circumstances, going on to refine our character into more Christlikeness as well. In turn, this process stirs up even greater hope in God. These transformations are what we should be focusing on rather than the trials in our lives. When we do, we not only better reflect Christ's character but we also give tribute to our Lord.

Thought to take:

Sometimes I get bombarded with invitations to join exclusive organizations that offer backstage access and all the perks that membership can provide. As you might imagine, almost every one of these offers involves paying a fee to take advantage of their benefits. Thankfully, God doesn't ask us to pay membership fees to be a part of His family. A mind-blowing thought, since we were the ones who ultimately nailed His Son to the cross! Honestly, we should be banned forever, yet God never takes access away from believers, no matter how badly we might fail Him. Instead, our justification is secure because we stand in Christ's righteousness rather than relying on our own good—though sub-par—merit.

Even though God's justification is free, it certainly is not cheap. God calls believers to walk where Jesus walked through sufferings and injustices for His sake. But even that is not a drawback since God uses every trouble and loss we face as a way to transform our character into Christlikeness. Whenever I experience suffering today, I will rely on God to help me stand strong in Him—thanking Him in advance for the endurance, character, and hope He is producing in me because of my faith in Him.

T2t: Rejoice in God's refinement

Help from the Lord: Pray for God's help to apply your T2t both now and all day long.

Father, even though I know it was Your love that provided a way for me to be justified through Christ, I also know that You didn't send Your Son to suffer and die for me just so I could live my life for my own desires and purposes. Yet You know how easy it is for me to let my desire for pleasure take over and, just as quickly, let the pain of this life distract and discourage me from following hard after You. So remind me that, through Christ, You give me the ability to stand in the middle of this tension. You give me the courage to focus on all the good You are doing but also strengthen me to stand steady and strong while under fire. So whenever I'm tempted to feel sorry for myself or try to evade pain through the pleasures of this life, open my eyes to Your exit plan—receiving Your grace in my time of need. Move me toward Christ so that I stand in Him, letting Him do His beautiful refining work on my heart and life through every trial. I promise to stop and consider all the ways You are helping me by developing endurance, character, and hope in my heart through Your grace. Thank You for making me a member of Your family and never revoking my membership no matter how weak I am or far I stray. Use this confidence and security to stir up more hope in You so that all will come to see my life as a tribute to Your Son! In Jesus' name, amen.

Yield to the Lord: Throughout the day, yield your way for God's way, prayerfully reflecting on how you did at the end of your day.

2 – A Love that Compels

Week 1, Day 2—Romans 5:5-8

Welcome the Lord!

> Open my eyes, that I may behold wondrous things out of your law.
> —Psalm 119:18

Observe what the Scripture says:

5 – and hope does not put us to shame, because God's love has been poured into our hearts through the Holy Spirit who has been given to us.
6 – For while we were still weak, at the right time Christ died for the ungodly.
7 – For one will scarcely die for a righteous person—though perhaps for a good person one would dare even to die—
8 – but God shows his love for us in that while we were still sinners, Christ died for us.

Recognize what is noteworthy and true:

Through the many trials and tribulations of our faith walk, God constantly works to produce not just endurance and character but also hope in our lives (v. 3-4). But here in verse 5, Paul identified what this hope does not produce and why, saying, **"and hope does not put us to shame, because God's love has been poured into our hearts through the Holy Spirit who has been given to us."** The phrase "does not put to shame" means that God's hope is never a disappointment. It is not hollow nor elusive. The reason for this is because God supplies His soul-satisfying love, pouring it into and filling up our hearts whenever we put our full hope in Him. The sufferings we experience in life can be the catalyst used by God to turn our hearts back to Him and His soul-drenching love.

In verse 6, Paul added yet another reality check for all believers, saying, **"For while we were still weak, at the right time Christ died for the ungodly."** Paul knew how easy it is for humans to think that we deserve or can earn this grace in our own strength. Ironically, humans can also feel as if they are too weak or defective for God to love and redeem. Still, we must remember that our weakness—our inability to earn salvation—actually makes God's work of redemption that much sweeter and more awe-inspiring. After all, Jesus loved us so much that He willingly came to die for the "ungodly"—those who rejected, sinned against, and killed Him. None of us can extricate ourselves from this equation and sin-problem. Every human is absolutely responsible for driving the nails into the hands and feet of Jesus. Amazingly, Christ offered Himself as the sacrifice that provides hope, love, and justification for everyone who trusts in Him.

In verses 7 and 8, Paul put this into greater perspective, saying: **"For one will scarcely die for a righteous person—though perhaps for a good person one would dare even to die—but God shows his love for us in that while we were still sinners, Christ died for us."** A "righteous person" is someone who lives uprightly, obeying God's word and law very closely and consistently. Paul then contrasted a righteous person with a "good person," referring to someone who not only lives according to God's word and law but does so from a good heart. We are much more inclined to die for someone who acts good or is good-hearted than someone who lives as closely as possible to the law, right? After all, the "righteous person" might also be self-righteous about his or her stellar obedience. Not a very endearing quality! Paul wanted to point out how God holds not only very different abilities but also different values from humans. Only God possesses the ability, strength, and motivation to show love for sinners. If we love those who have sinned against us, it is only because God has provided and empowered that love to flow in and through us, making it not only transformational but also miraculous.

Thought to take:

This reading declares two truths and realities Christ-followers must embrace. The first truth highlights the love God pours into every believer's heart. The love of God not only personally helps us feel secure and accepted by Him, but it also empowers us to love others with the love He pours into our hearts. That's quite the encouragement and transformation! Amazingly, the second truth seems to go further—jumping off the page like someone doing a cannonball into a deep pool, splashing the love of God onto everyone within reach! That's because this second truth shows the depths to which God's love compelled Him to go for us—dying for us while we were still sinners. We must consider all the ways that the Father and Son have sacrificed for us or we will take for granted His love. But by remembering and celebrating God's love and sacrifices, our hearts will overflow with His love for others, sacrificing for them like our Savior did for us. So, not only will I meditate on the depths of God's love for me—thanking Him for each one—but I will also dedicate this day to showering others with the overflowing love of God through Christ-like sacrifices.

T2t: Know and show God's love

Help **from the Lord:** Pray for God's help to apply your T2t both now and all day long.

> *Father, what great love You and Your Son show to those unworthy of Your love ... to those who sin against You day-after-day. I was one of those ungodly and weak souls that You saw and loved long before I was born. You reached out to me from the cross with the only love that could awaken me, saving me from my sins. Let me never forget how unfair and excruciating it was for Your Son to take on my shame and blame—being mocked, scourged, and crucified, all so I could be Your child. May I also never forget how costly Jesus' sacrifice was nor how amazing it is to stand before You with Christ's righteousness covering my shame. But what touches me most is how You pour Your love into my heart every single day! Enable me to remember that I cannot conjure up Your love in my own strength, nor can my heart contain all the love You pour into it. Your love overflows from my heart and is meant to be poured onto others. Do not ever let me keep Your love all to myself, instead I must freely extend it to all who do not deserve love of any kind, much less, Your love. Remind me to consider how much You sacrificed for me, using that to convince me of how deep Your love is for me. I know this will move me to show love to all I encounter, including those who are weak, sinful, and broken. After all, that's how far Your love went for me—Your weak child, made strong by my Savior! In Jesus' name, amen.*

Yield **to the Lord:** Throughout the day, yield your way for God's way, prayerfully reflecting on how you did at the end of your day.

3 – The Many Sides of God's Love

Week 1, Day 3—Romans 5:9-11

Welcome the Lord!

Open my eyes, that I may behold wondrous things out of your law.
—Psalm 119:18

Observe what the Scripture says:

9 – Since, therefore, we have now been justified by his blood, much more shall we be saved by him from the wrath of God.
10 – For if while we were enemies we were reconciled to God by the death of his Son, much more, now that we are reconciled, shall we be saved by his life.
11 – More than that, we also rejoice in God through our Lord Jesus Christ, through whom we have now received reconciliation.

Recognize what is noteworthy and true:

Paul laid a foundation of how God's grace—through Christ—benefits and helps the redeemed in this chapter. But today, in verse 9, he would add another very important benefit and by-product, saying, **"Since, therefore, we have now been justified by his blood, much more shall we be saved by him from the wrath of God."** In order for God to be God and true to His righteous, holy, and just character, He had to deal with our sin problem. It would actually be unloving of God to ignore our sin since sin damages and destroys us. Thankfully, believers are seen by the Father as innocent because our sinless, innocent Savior's blood covers our sin, allowing us to escape the justified wrath and punishment of God. This verse contrasts the tough side of God's love with the unconditional, unfathomable, and unlimited side of His love.

In verse 10, Paul puts this awe-inspiring outcome into perspective with these words, **"For if while we were enemies we were reconciled to God by the death of his Son, much more, now that we are reconciled, shall we be saved by his life."** Before Christ reconciled us to Himself, our sin made us His enemies. We can foolishly rail against God's wrath, yet we were the ones, in our unredeemed state, who chose to wage war against Him. We were the ones rejecting Him and His ways while embracing our own. If Scripture reveals this to us now, should we expect the just Judge to let us off the hook or look the other way? Thankfully, God devised a plan involving His Son sacrificing His life, with Christ lovingly taking on the sentence and punishment that we, as guilty sinners (criminals, really), deserved. In this way, God could reconcile or accept us to Himself—taking us from hostile enemy to pardoned sinner and beloved family member. The final thought in this verse reminds us that being saved through Jesus' death gives us an even greater assurance that He will keep us saved by and through His life. Now that Christ is our living Redeemer—having triumphed over sin and the grave— we can also trust Him to sustain our reconciliation or faithfulness to God through His resurrection power. Jesus empowers us to live for Him—our living Savior— every day of our lives.

In verse 11, Paul gladly declared: **"More than that, we also rejoice in God through our Lord Jesus Christ, through whom we have now received reconciliation."** We have every reason to rejoice since we are justified—saved from God's wrath and saved through Christ's life. Some translations use the word "atonement" for reconciliation here, highlighting how our reconciliation comes because of Christ's atoning sacrifice. Think of atonement like this—it is "at-one-ment." Christ's atonement makes us one with God. This verse also says we receive reconciliation and are not the ones reaching out to reconcile with God. In one sense, we do not "accept Jesus" as much as God accepts us through and because of the saving work of Christ. Through our faith in Christ, we become recipients of the gift that keeps on giving.

Thought to take:

Most of the time, the gifts we give to other people serve one or maybe two purposes at most. That's why God's gift of salvation is so amazing! Just some of the many benefits we receive from God are justification from sin through Christ's death, freedom from God's wrath, reconciliation with God, and salvation through Christ's life. But God's gift also reflects all the multifaceted and generous sides of the "love" of our Lord. Thinking about these benefits and what they cost Jesus will certainly compel us to rejoice, stirring even greater thankfulness in our hearts. So whenever I feel lonely or afraid today, I will remember that, through Christ, I am made right with God. I'm no longer His enemy! Through Christ's atonement I am made one with God. I am never really alone! And when I feel like I can't make it through some problem, I will remember and reach out for Christ's resurrection and saving power. I have all I need to live for Jesus.

T2t: Recall and rely on God's benefits

Help **from the Lord:** Pray for God's help to apply your T2t both now and all day long.

> *Father, Your love is so much deeper, richer, and more multi-faceted than I could ever imagine. It is not only a lavish love but a perfect love for every need in my life. That's why I'm so grateful Your Son willingly paid the price for the bottomless debt I owe You. Jesus' blood covers the despicable and depraved ways I sin against You—assuring me of justification. But Your Son's sacrifice also enables me to experience this bountiful gift of justification in a variety of ways. This makes it a gift that I can unwrap every single day and in all sorts of ways. As I do that today, remind me of all Christ endured for my sake so that I will rejoice in Him no matter the trouble or strife I face. Go further to remind me of how wonderful it is that Your Son satisfied Your wrath, removing the sting of death from me through Jesus my Redeemer! Enable me to not only consider all the ways You have broken down the barrier between sinners—drawing me to Yourself—but also encourage me with this thought whenever I feel lonely or outnumbered. For, with You, I am never alone! Your Son is alive and, through the Spirit, walks beside me, living within me, giving me the power to live for You at every turn. Encourage my heart with all of these benefits, Lord. Make my faith stronger, letting my love for You shine brighter because of all You have done to prove Your love to me. In Christ's name, amen.*

Yield **to the Lord:** Throughout the day, yield your way for God's way, prayerfully reflecting on how you did at the end of your day.

Week One Questions for Discussion or Contemplation

Read aloud Day 1, Romans 5:1-4 ...

1. Why do you think God doesn't give access to the justification of Christ to everyone (vv. 1-2)? What problems would occur if He left it wide open no matter our response to Christ?

2. How has God used sufferings in your life to produce endurance, character, hope (vv. 3-4)? How often do you meditate on this?

3. What are the truths or truth principles we might not have talked about yet from verses 1-4 that catch your attention, and why?

Read aloud Day 2, Romans 5:5-8 ...

4. If God's love has been poured into the hearts of believers, why do we sometimes struggle with shame (v. 5)? To love others? What can we do to better recognize this problem? Resolve it?

5. What are some extensions and benefits of this truth—that Christ died for the "weak" and "ungodly" (v. 6)? In other words, why didn't Jesus die for the strong and godly?

6. What are the truths or truth principles we might not have talked about yet from verses 5-8 that catch your attention, and why?

Read aloud Day 3, Romans 5:9-11 ...

7. What are the blessings, found in verses 9-11, of being justified by Christ? (Write them down!) How can or does meditating on these benefits improve your attitude and strengthen your faith regarding a particular trouble in your life.

8. What are the truths or truth principles we might not have talked about yet from verses 9-11 that catch your attention, and why?

9. What is one thing from this past week's study that you want to learn from and live out more?

10. Would anyone like to read a prayer you wrote based on one of the Scriptures from this week? How can we pray for you?

Week Two

4 – From Man to Son of Man

Week 2, Day 1—Romans 5:12-14

Welcome the Lord!

> Open my eyes, that I may behold wondrous things out of your law.
> —Psalm 119:18

Observe what the Scripture says:

12 – Therefore, just as sin came into the world through one man, and death through sin, and so death spread to all men because all sinned—
13 – for sin indeed was in the world before the law was given, but sin is not counted where there is no law.
14 – Yet death reigned from Adam to Moses, even over those whose sinning was not like the transgression of Adam, who was a type of the one who was to come.

Recognize what is noteworthy and true:

Paul unpacked more reasons why we need to be justified and reconciled to God in today's passage, adding: **"Therefore, just as sin came into the world through one man, and death through sin, and so death spread to all men because all sinned—"** (v. 12). This statement clarifies that the entry point for sin came through "one man," meaning Adam, and establishes the harsh reality that we are all born with a sin nature (Ps. 51:5; Rom. 3:23). Although Eve sinned before Adam, she was deceived by the serpent to sin. In contrast, Adam knew exactly what he was doing when he sinned (1 Tim. 2:14). As the head of his household and father of mankind, God required more of Adam and placed the blame squarely at his feet. Paul then explained how death came into the world and "spread to all men," referring to how all humans are born spiritually dead because of the sin nature. We will all die physically and those who reject Christ's salvation will die eternally (be condemned to hell). Thankfully, believers are made spiritually alive in Christ at salvation, enabling us, after we physically die, to live with God in heaven forever.

In verse 13, Paul continued on to say, **"for sin indeed was in the world before the law was given, but sin is not counted where there is no law."** Adam chose to sin long before God gave the law to humans. Sin entered the world at that point through Adam and his offspring (mankind), with humans inheriting a sin nature. So, does the second half of this verse really mean that God did not count the sins of those who sinned before the law was given? Yes and no. Yes, God did not count them as "sinners" or law-breakers because they did not know the law yet. But this does not mean that humans can escape the physical and spiritual consequences of death brought on by our sins since verse 12 makes no such distinction. The punishment still stood even though humans, at that point, lacked the awful title of "sinners."

In verse 14, Paul further fleshed out what Adam represented when he said, **"Yet death reigned from Adam to Moses, even over those whose sinning was not like the transgression of Adam, who was a type of the one who was to come."** Adam was a type (representation of) and contrast "to the one who was to come"—representing Christ. Both Adam and Christ were sinless men; Adam at the start of his life and Jesus from beginning to end. Because Adam sinned, death reigned over all mankind from his time onward. Ultimately, none of us can escape the rule and reign that physical death holds over our bodies, completely succumbing to it one day whether we like it or not. When Paul said, "even over those whose sinning was not like the transgression of Adam," he was saying that everyone is without excuse. We cannot say, "Well, my sin is not as bad as Adam's, so I'm off the hook!" If we sin in the smallest of ways, we are guilty and in need of the atonement of Christ.

Thought to take:

Even though Adam was ultimately responsible for committing the first sin— passing sin down to all of his offspring (mankind)—we all are still held responsible for the sins we commit. We all are guilty of sin and deserve the punishment that results in physical and spiritual death. Thankfully, that's not where God allowed the story to end. Even though Adam was a sinful type, representing man or mankind; Christ came as our representative to redeem the lost as the sinless Son of Man. I never want to lose sight of what my sin cost Jesus nor take for granted the triumph this provides for me—for all who place their faith in Him! So, throughout this day, I will thank God for overcoming the reign of sin in my life, giving me the strength to resist temptation and obey Him. I will also thank Jesus for breaking the grip of death, enabling me to not only live with spiritual abundance now but also forever with Him in eternity one day.

T2t: Jesus broke death's grip!

Help from the Lord: Pray for God's help to apply your T2t both now and all day long.

Father, I know that I take my salvation and the price Christ paid for my sin for granted far too often. Yet, Your Son cured me of a horrific and deadly sin disease, passed down to me through my ancestor Adam! Without Your cure, this disease would have thrown me into the deepest pit of hell. A place where not even the flames can inflict the worst kind of torture. No! The worst part would have been spending my eternity separated from You! Thank You for sparing me that horrific fate through Your Son's sacrifice. And thank You for indulging me now with so great a life through Your Son, not to mention, my life with You after I die! Help me contemplate today all that this means, all that Your Son has done and won for me—breaking the grip of death and sin. Winning a place for me before Your throne in the glories of heaven! Use this deepening realization to create a stronger appreciation for Your salvation, deepening my love for my Savior as well. How can I not thank You all day long—all life long—for this precious gift? Forgive me for not really grappling with it more often and more profoundly. Instead, let today be the start of a new habit and greater recognition of all Your redemption means for me. Thank You, once again, for enduring all that Your Son's sacrifice involved and meant for You as His loving Father. Please, know that I love You with all my heart! In Christ's name, amen.

Yield to the Lord: Throughout the day, yield your way for God's way, prayerfully reflecting on how you did at the end of your day.

5 – What's Lost and Gained

Week 2, Day 2—Romans 5:15-17

Welcome the Lord!

Open my eyes, that I may behold wondrous things out of your law.
—Psalm 119:18

Observe what the Scripture says:

15 – But the free gift is not like the trespass. For if many died through one man's trespass, much more have the grace of God and the free gift by the grace of that one man Jesus Christ abounded for many.
16 – And the free gift is not like the result of that one man's sin. For the judgment following one trespass brought condemnation, but the free gift following many trespasses brought justification.
17 – For if, because of one man's trespass, death reigned through that one man, much more will those who receive the abundance of grace and the free gift of righteousness reign in life through the one man Jesus Christ.

Recognize what is noteworthy and true:

Paul laid out more contrasts for us between the sinful Adam and the sinless Christ in verse 15a, starting with, **"But the free gift is not like the trespass."** The free gift of God's grace and the "trespass" (offense) that humans commit against God and His law represents opposite ends of a continuum. On one end, man's sin and rebellion (through Adam) are highlighted along with the deadly consequences. On the other end, Christ's holiness and redemptive power are displayed and offered to those who trust in Him.

In verse 15b, Paul then juxtaposed the effect of one man's sin on many with God's solution for the many: **"For if many died through one man's trespass, much more have the grace of God and the free gift by the grace of that one man Jesus Christ abounded for many."** The first sin Adam committed in the Garden allowed the curse of death to rain down on and reign in the hearts of "many"—all humans. But God did not allow that consequence to overrule the free gift of His grace nor to defeat His redemptive plan for the many who believe(d). The grace of God triumphs here. His grace is much more abounding and abundant through the "one man Jesus Christ" for us than the trespass is destructive and deadly to us. It's as if what we lost, through the sins we've all committed, cannot come close to all that we gain through the grace of God, made possible by Christ.

In verse 16, Paul reemphasized this crucial point: **"the free gift is not like the result of that one man's sin. For the judgment following one trespass brought condemnation, but the free gift following many trespasses brought justification."** Like 15a, here in verse 16a, Paul contrasted the one trespass that brought condemnation on Adam and all of mankind with the free gift that provides Christ's justification. Amazingly, this justification is guaranteed and stays in place even after we commit many trespasses and sins. This truth showcases the lasting power of God's grace for those He redeems, including all the endless times His grace covers the many times we sin as believers during our lifetimes.

In verse 17, Paul offered further nuance to this far-reaching impact of God's grace: **"For if, because of one man's trespass, death reigned through that one man, much more will those who receive the abundance of grace and the free gift of righteousness reign in life through the one man Jesus Christ."** Thankfully, Jesus—as "the one man"—broke the reign of death, which came through "that one man" (Adam). Now, believers are empowered to reign in life through the abundant grace and righteousness of Christ. Through Christ, we are abundantly blessed with the life-igniting, life-transforming, and life-enriching power of His grace each day. God and His grace help us to live triumphantly each day for the one man who matters most—Jesus.

Thought to take:

When Adam sinned and God ushered him out of the Garden of Eden, all hope seemed lost. Sadly, Adam was not the only one who lost hope. We all lost hope since every human follows Adam's pattern into sin, giving in to lives stained by sin from our birth onward. It's as if God puts up a "No Trespassing" sign, revealing where we should walk in life based on His law and word. Yet this does not keep us from constantly stepping over the boundary lines God reveals to us. Thankfully, Jesus was willing to step in as our Advocate to save us—to be the one man who could pay the price for our trespasses, giving us His grace to overcome sin. So today, I want to consider how much was lost when sin entered the world. I also want to remember and focus on the abundance that Jesus gained back for me as His redeemed child. He now makes what I gain through His grace so much more abundant and powerful than what I lost when I was unrepentant and dead in my sins. I will keep my mind on these contrasting truths today, meditating mostly on all I gain because of Christ's salvation and His gift of grace upon grace.

T2t: Think on all I gain in Christ

Help from the Lord: Pray for God's help to apply your T2t both now and all day long.

> Father, this passage showcases the worst and best outcome of Your redemption story. The harsh and dismal side of the story begins with Adam and, ultimately, all the human race choosing to go our own way. We all have trespassed beyond Your boundary lines—crossing lines that offend You and destroy us. Thankfully, this story also showcases the sweet and triumphant sacrifice of Jesus, my Savior! Your Son saw me wandering in the fields of rebellion and corruption. Jesus knew the danger I was in before I could see the destruction heading my way. Christ knew what I needed even before I knew I needed His help. But those hindrances did not matter nor get in You or Your Son's way! Your grace that now envelopes me is so amazing! What joy I feel knowing that Jesus is my Lord and Savior! Still, You give me so much more through Your grace than the best outcome—my salvation! How can it be? Your grace not only saves me from sin, death, and the flames of hell but also saves me in every trial and trouble that comes my way. Thank You for giving me back much more than I lost by cancelling the curse of sin. Keep on using Your grace to help conform, encourage, and strengthen me so that I will live each day for Your Son—the one Man who blesses me in every possible way! In Jesus' name, amen.

Yield to the Lord: Throughout the day, yield your way for God's way, prayerfully reflecting on how you did at the end of your day.

6 – God's Grace is Greater

Week 2, Day 3—Romans 5:18-21

Welcome the Lord!

Open my eyes, that I may behold wondrous things out of your law.
—Psalm 119:18

Observe what the Scripture says:

18 – Therefore, as one trespass led to condemnation for all men, so one act of righteousness leads to justification and life for all men.
19 – For as by the one man's disobedience the many were made sinners, so by the one man's obedience the many will be made righteous.
20 – Now the law came in to increase the trespass, but where sin increased, grace abounded all the more,
21 – so that, as sin reigned in death, grace also might reign through righteousness leading to eternal life through Jesus Christ our Lord.

Recognize what is noteworthy and true:

As this chapter comes to a close, Paul notes the parallel between Adam and Christ once more in verse 18: **"Therefore, as one trespass led to condemnation for all men, so one act of righteousness leads to justification and life for all men."** Even though Paul gave us the worst news at the start, he followed it up with the best news—our hope in Christ! The one trespass or sin that Adam committed in the garden resulted in condemnation for all of mankind. Nevertheless, Christ's one "act of righteousness"—giving His sinless life on the cross—triumphed over this trespass and condemnation. His gracious act leads and draws us to receive "justification and life" through Him.

In verse 19, Paul further discussed how the choices of Adam and Christ impacted the "many:" **"For as by the one man's disobedience the many were made sinners, so by the one man's obedience the many will be made righteous."** Through the one man's (Adam's) disobedience and sin, many—meaning "all" (Rom. 5:20; 3:10; 3:23, etc.)—have been made sinners. But through the one man's (Christ's) obedience, "many" will be made righteous. Not all people are made righteous by God, but rather all can respond to the opportunity to "be made righteous" through Christ. And when this happens, many are justified.

Paul again started off with the bad news in verse 20, saying, **"Now the law came in to increase the trespass,"** adding both the human response to the law and the divine one—**"but where sin increased, grace abounded all the more,".** This verse tells us that God's law increases the results or evidence of sin since it reveals where His boundary lines are. Paul then highlighted how humans respond to the law, stepping over these boundary lines into sinful territory time and time again. But even God's reason for giving us the law—to expose our sin (Rom. 7:7)—is a gracious one since it helps us recognize our need for Him. Furthermore, God's response to our dilemma, brought on by the law, showcases the greater grace of God. His grace abounded "all the more" in ways that cover our sinful and shameful disobedience, making His grace greater than the worst sinner's sin.

Paul concluded with a final parallel between man's sin and God's grace, saying, **"so that, as sin reigned in death, grace also might reign through righteousness leading to eternal life through Jesus Christ our Lord"** (v. 21). Before a person receives Christ, sin reigns in his or her life, bringing spiritual, physical, and eternal death. Thankfully, Christ's gift of grace offers freedom from this life-stealing slavery to sin and eternal damnation. We still all must physically die one day but when we surrender our earthly lives to Jesus, His Spirit comes to reign within us. Through our new life in Christ, He also gives us abundant grace, helping us resist sin now and guaranteeing our eternal life with Him in the hereafter.

Thought to take:

Movies nowadays hardly ever depict a happy ending. I think that's likely because there are very few happy endings in life without some degree of loss, evil, or disappointment involved. Thankfully, God was unwilling to stand by and watch people living out their brief lives as slaves to sin and death. Instead, the one man—Jesus—stepped into our fallen world, holding all the power to reverse the curse and offering the justification we need to stand clothed in His righteousness. As one of the many that Christ redeemed, this inspires me to praise Him for bearing my shame and punishment so that I'm no longer controlled by sin or mired in condemnation. It also stirs my gratitude for all the abounding and abundant ways His grace is greater than my sin. He fills up my life with meaning and joy not only now but also provides a heavenly home where joys will never cease! With all of this in mind, I will praise and worship the Lord for the multitude of ways He turned this bleak and hopeless story and outcome around for me—for all the redeemed—with His triumphal redemption and grace.

T2t: Praise God for His great grace

Help from the Lord: Pray for God's help to apply your T2t both now and all day long.

> *Father, there are countless ways that sin has infiltrated my life through the one man—Adam. Yet there are also countless ways that Your grace, through the One man—Jesus—has overcome sin and the tragic outcomes my depraved choices have brought. Thank You that I never have to walk covered in shame since Christ bore that shame for me on the cursed tree. And I never have to bow to sin or let it control my life because Christ now reigns in my heart. Your Son assures me the victory over every sin and temptation this life can throw at me. Help me look each day to Your law so that I not only see where I've gotten off course but also know how to live a life that honors You. And never let me view that same law as a way to gain Your acceptance or righteousness. I know without a doubt that Christ is the only One who was able to achieve that impossible goal. May I spend this day reaching out for Christ's greater grace—the grace that triumphed over all of my sins. I also will spend it thanking You for every way Your grace helps, strengthens, and enriches my life. Drive Your grace deeper into my heart so that all people see is a greater reflection of Your Son, overcoming, once again, all that is broken, hopeless, and shameful in me. In Jesus' name, amen.*

Yield to the Lord: Throughout the day, yield your way for God's way, prayerfully reflecting on how you did at the end of your day.

Week Two Questions for Discussion or Contemplation

Read aloud Day 1, Romans 5:12-14 ...

1. Why do you think God held Adam responsible for the spread of death and sin to all since Eve also sinned (v. 12)?

2. Why do you think God did not count sin when people did not yet have the law (13)? What does that tell you about His character?

3. Why do you think it's so tempting to compare our sins with others, thinking ours are not as bad (v. 14)? What can help prevent this kind of tendency or mindset?

4. What are the truths or truth principles we might not have talked about yet from verses 12-14 that catch your attention, and why?

Read aloud Day 2, Romans 5:15-17 ...

5. How hard is it for you to remain secure in the reality of your justification whenever you sin (v. 16)? How can this verse help you resist feeling constantly condemned?

6. What are some of the additional blessings (abundance of grace) you have received from Christ and His free gift of salvation (v. 17)?

7. Where do you think you would be if you had not received Christ's free gift?

8. What are the truths or truth principles we might not have talked about yet from verses 15-17 that catch your attention, and why?

Read aloud Day 3, Romans 5:18-21 ...

9. What do you think it means to "be made righteous" (v. 19)?

10. What are obvious ways that we, as believers, can let the reign of Christ's righteousness show up more in our lives (v. 21)?

11. What are the truths or truth principles we might not have talked about yet from verses 18-21 that catch your attention, and why?

12. What is one thing from this past week's study that you want to learn from and live out more?

13. Would anyone like to read a prayer you wrote based on one of the Scriptures from this week? How can we pray for you?

Week Three

7 – Grace Taken for Granted?

Week 3, Day 1—Romans 6:1-3

Welcome the Lord!

Open my eyes, that I may behold wondrous things out of your law.
—Psalm 119:18

Observe what the Scripture says:

1 – What shall we say then? Are we to continue in sin that grace may abound?
2 – By no means! How can we who died to sin still live in it?
3 – Do you not know that all of us who have been baptized into Christ Jesus were baptized into his death?

Recognize what is noteworthy and true:

In Romans 5, Paul gave attention to the many blessed outcomes of being justified through our faith in Christ. But here in chapter 6, the words from Romans 5:20—"where sin increased, grace abounded all the more"—must have continued to echo in Paul's mind. So in verse 1, he continued this line of thought by posing two related questions: **"What shall we say then? Are we to continue in sin that grace may abound?"** The meaning behind the Greek word for "sin" here points to sins that are habitual, forming a lifestyle. Paul surely knew how tempting it would be to take unfair advantage of the abounding grace of God by giving ourselves permission to sin. But just because God's grace abounds does not mean we have the freedom to rebel against Him. After all, He gave His life to redeem our sins and continuously extends this costly grace to us all day long each day.

In verse 2, Paul answered his own question—**"By no means!"**—following it up with, **"How can we who died to sin still live in it?"** This question reminds us to never take the grace of God for granted by choosing to sin or living a sinful lifestyle. Bible Scholar, Dr. Thomas Constable, offers further perspective on what Paul was saying, adding that living in sin is like a widow continuing to live as if her husband is still alive. No one in their right mind would do that. Thankfully, not only does Christ give believers the power to die to sin (the old, unfaithful spouse) but His grace also covers every trespass we commit. Still, you and I must never forget that our sins grieve the Holy Spirit (Eph. 4:30). And if we sin continuously, we will suppress or quench the Holy Spirit within us (1 Thes. 5:19), resulting in greater spiritual wandering, sinful choices, and hardness of heart.

In verse 3, Paul added another reason believers cannot choose to live in sin, rhetorically asking, **"Do you not know that all of us who have been baptized into Christ Jesus were baptized into his death?"** The word "baptized" here involves the idea of being immersed and covered over with something. When we place our faith in Christ, He forgives and covers our sin (4:7), baptizing or immersing us in His righteousness. When believers are baptized, they follow the example Jesus set when He submitted to baptism (even though Christ did not need baptism). Through baptism, believers give an outward sign of the inward change our faith in Christ has made. Laying back and being covered with water represents both Christ's death and our death to our former sinful lives. When we are raised out of the water, it showcases Christ's resurrection and our new life in Him.

Interestingly, Paul began talking about those who died to sin (v. 2) before saying they "were baptized" (v. 3), alluding to the fact that the act of baptism does not save us. Another important verse supporting this comes from the Apostle Peter when said in Acts 2:38, "Repent and be baptized" rather than be baptized so you can repent. (For further evidence that it is faith in Christ and not baptism that saves us, see 1 Cor. 1:17; Lk. 23:42; Acts 9:17-18; Rom. 10:9.) Another way that a believer's life is baptized or symbolically covered is with suffering (Mt. 16:24). Our call to follow Christ involves dying to self (being baptized into His death) and taking up our crosses so that Christ lives through us.

Thought to take:

Even though God's grace abounds in the life of everyone who receives Christ's salvation, it is not something we should ever take for granted. An exchange took place when we placed our faith in Christ, exchanging our lives for Christ's, with God baptizing (symbolically immersing) us into Christ's death. From the point of our salvation onward, we are to die to our former sinful lives, letting Jesus' will and desires override our will and desires at every tempting turn in our day. I will take up this challenge by resisting choices that feed my desires, pursuing instead what honors Christ. I will also make a point of thanking Jesus throughout this day for His grace and gift of salvation, yielding my way for His whenever my human desires cry out to be fulfilled.

T2t: Thank Jesus and yield to Him

Help from the Lord: Pray for God's help to apply your T2t both now and all day long.

> Father, I am so grateful that Your grace abounds because I desperately need it for my salvation. I also need it for every difficulty in this life. So I praise Jesus for being willing to die, allowing me to live through Him. What a glorious and paradoxical exchange—finding the best life through dying to myself and living for Christ alone! As I go about this day, I will take time to contemplate all that Your Son did to make this exchange possible so that I avoid taking Your grace for granted. In the good and bad moments of this day, I will rejoice and worship You for all You provide for me through Christ's grace and gift of salvation. I will dedicate this day to thanking Jesus for the price He paid for my redemption—for my new life in You. And when I'm tempted to focus on myself, trying to find satisfaction or accomplishment apart from You, empower me to resist these temptations and foolish idols. Convict and bring me back quickly to the place where true satisfaction is found—in You and You alone. My life is Yours, dear Father! Do with it whatever You desire today and every day! In Jesus' name, amen.

Yield to the Lord: Throughout the day, yield your way for God's way, prayerfully reflecting on how you did at the end of your day.

8 – United in Death and Life

Week 3, Day 2—Romans 6:4-5

Welcome the Lord!

Open my eyes, that I may behold wondrous things out of your law.
—Psalm 119:18

Observe what the Scripture says:

4 – We were buried therefore with him by baptism into death, in order that, just as Christ was raised from the dead by the glory of the Father, we too might walk in newness of life.
5 – For if we have been united with him in a death like his, we shall certainly be united with him in a resurrection like his.

Recognize what is noteworthy and true:

In the reading for yesterday, Paul laid down the challenge for us not to take God's grace for granted—choosing to sin or live in sin (v. 2). In verse 3, Paul gives us the foundational reason and irrefutable fact for why this understanding is so important—if we've "been baptized into Christ," we've also been "baptized into his death."

However, in the Scripture for today, Paul went further, explaining why being baptized into Christ's death is such a necessary part of redemption for believers. He added in verse 4, **"We were buried therefore with him by baptism into death, in order that, just as Christ was raised from the dead by the glory of the Father, we too might walk in newness of life."** Paul not only pointed out the spiritual reality of baptism in a believer's life (v. 3), but he also emphasized the picture of what baptism represents in verse 4—Christ's death and resurrection.

First, the act of baptism illustrates and gives testimony of how a person has chosen to die to sin—being laid back and covered like we are dead. Second, this verse explains that those who place their faith in Christ actually participate in His death. In a spiritual sense, believers have been laid in the grave with Jesus. But then, just as Christ was raised from the dead, God raises up every believer spiritually to "walk in newness of life," enabling us to also participate in Jesus' resurrection! We not only die to sin and the sinful lifestyles we lived in before coming to Christ, but we also are made spiritually alive with Him. God broke the power of the sinful nature for those who are redeemed, giving us the ability—through Christ—to resist sin when we rely on Him. Paul also highlighted and declared here how this gloriously demonstrates God's power to save and sanctify the redeemed. Again, I believe that God does not save us through the act of baptism but rather saves us by grace (Eph. 2:8), secured for believers through Christ's sacrificial death and resurrection.

In verse 5, Paul elaborated on what being baptized into Christ's death and resurrection leads to, saying, **"For if we have been united with him in a death like his, we shall certainly be united with him in a resurrection like his."** Paul's terminology here—"we have been united with him"—depicts the inseparable union between believers and Christ. It also captures the idea of being grafted into the life of something like a tree or plant. When God grafts us into Christ, He separates us from our old life (sin/sinful lifestyles) and joins us into the life of Christ. He then nourishes believers, enabling us to resemble Him—the One we are grafted into for sustenance. Paul also shifted focus here from our spiritual resurrection (v. 4) to the physical resurrection of believers (v. 5). Paul used a particular sentence structure in the Greek, using the future tense of "we shall be" (v. 5) to reveal another encouraging fact about our new life in Christ. One day our Lord will return for the redeemed. On that day, every believer shall be bodily resurrected and united with Christ in the glories of heaven.

Thought to take:

We cannot overlook how Paul clarified a very encouraging truth for us here. He reminded us of just how united believers are with Christ. The redeemed are not just united with Jesus in His death and resurrection but will also be united with Him one day when He comes again to resurrect and raise our bodies. If we remember these glorious realities, it will help us live our lives for Christ alone. Since we have died to sin, we should never try to unite Christ with a "corpse," essentially returning to our former lives, letting sin control us. We must also remember that God resurrected believers just as much as He raised Jesus on that glorious third day, enabling us to walk in newness of life. In other words, we have Christ's resurrection power available at all times to us, enabling us to overcome every temptation. Finally, we must look forward to the day when Christ will come for us, resurrecting and raising us to life with God in the glorious throne room of heaven. So I will strive to remember that I am not my own but Christ's alone. I will rely on Him for His resurrection power and rejoice in the amazing truth that I will join Him forever in heaven one day.

T2t: Walk with Jesus and rejoice in Him

Help from the Lord: Pray for God's help to apply your T2t both now and all day long.

> *Jesus, Your love and power are so multifaceted and awe-inspiring! You rescued me from my former life—steeped in sinful and corrupt choices. You allowed me to not only die with You in Your tomb but have raised me to new life through Your resurrection power. Just mindboggling! What You accomplished on the cross defeated the sin that would have slain and left me without hope—separated from You. Thankfully, death, sin, and this impossible mission for anyone else could not keep You down. Deepen my understanding and appreciation for this miraculous victory and mysterious union I now have with You—that can never be severed or taken away. Use these glorious truths to keep me steady, walking by Your side, and going wherever You walk. Always empower me to wield Your resurrection power whenever I am tempted to sin or give up. In those weak moments, remind me that You have already won the victory, and I only need to keep walking it out in Your power while keeping my eyes focused on Your return. Thank You for being there for me, for redeeming my sinful past, for sanctifying and sustaining me not only in the present but also uniting me with You forever in the future! In Your name, amen.*

Yield to the Lord: Throughout the day, yield your way for God's way, prayerfully reflecting on how you did at the end of your day.

9 – Slain and Set Free

Week 3, Day 3—Romans 6:6-8

Welcome the Lord!

> Open my eyes, that I may behold wondrous things out of your law.
> —Psalm 119:18

Observe what the Scripture says:

6 – We know that our old self was crucified with him in order that the body of sin might be brought to nothing, so that we would no longer be enslaved to sin.
7 – For one who has died has been set free from sin.
8 – Now if we have died with Christ, we believe that we will also live with him.

Recognize what is noteworthy and true:

In today's text, Paul continued to explain the mystery of how believers "have been united with Christ" in His death and resurrection (v. 5). However, in this section of Scripture, he highlighted a slightly different and more subtle component of the redemption story.

In verse 6, Paul said, **"We know that our old self was crucified with him in order that the body of sin might be brought to nothing, so that we would no longer be enslaved to sin."** In my studies of this text, most Bible scholars assert that the "old self" is not the same as the sin nature or flesh. These theologians believe Paul would have used the terminology sin nature or flesh (Rom. 7:14; 7:25; 8:13) both here and elsewhere if the old self and flesh were one and the same. Instead, Paul strategically chose to say "old self" or "old things" in places where the context supported a different meaning like it does here (see also 2 Cor. 5:17; Eph. 4:22; Col. 3:9).

The old self represents our former sinful lives, when we operated totally independent of God. Paul's question in verse 2 clarifies the state of the old self—the old self of the believer has "died to sin" the moment a believer places his or her faith in Christ. Spiritually speaking, a believer's former sinful life was vicariously crucified with Christ when Jesus died on the cross, bringing "the body of sin" to nothing through the Savior's death. As believers, we must constantly remind ourselves that the body of sin is nothing—is dead. It cannot force us to sin any longer. Still, as long as we are in the body, we will feel the pull to sin because our "sin nature" is still active, though we are no longer enslaved to it. Therefore, we must submit to the reign and power of Christ each day, remembering our old lives have passed away and Christ has made us new creations in Him (2 Cor. 5:17).

In verse 7, Paul reiterated his last triumphant point for emphasis, saying, **"For one who has died has been set free from sin."** When Christ was crucified, He crucified the old self of believers and broke the power of the sin nature (our enslavement to sin), enabling us to resist sins of every kind in His power. This means the believer's "old self" is dead and gone and, through Christ, we have been set free from the domination of the sin nature even as it still rises up to tempt us.

In verse 8, Paul focused once again on what salvation produces in the lives of believers, saying, **"Now if we have died with Christ, we believe that we will also live with him."** It's important to note that the Greek word used here for "if" can also be translated "since," reflecting a certainty of fact. It is a certain fact that Christ-followers have died with Christ. But what is equally true is the fact that we will live with Christ one day. Since Paul stated this with the phrase "we will," indicating a future point in time, likely alluding to the day we will die when God frees us from our physical bodies and sin natures. This idea also circles back to what Paul shared in verse 5 regarding the return of Christ to resurrect believers one day. Whether this points to the life we will one day live with Jesus in heaven or speaks of the abundant life we experience in Him here and now—one thing is for sure: as Christ-followers, we are inseparably linked and unified with Christ now and forever.

Thought to take:

Paul has given believers every challenge to leave our former ways of living behind, closing the casket and burying them in the ground. Why has He done that? Because, when we are in Christ, our former lives are dead and gone! We shouldn't try to visit, in a figurative sense, the graveside of our old lives with flowers in hand, reminiscing about all the "good times" we had when we were living in sin. As Christ-followers, we should continually focus our hope and attention on the freedom and life Christ has already given us who are redeemed. So when temptations come my way today, I will remember the freedom I have in Christ to say no to the old and yes to the new. The chains of slavery, sin, and death no longer hold me captive. I will rely on Christ to help me resist every temptation, trusting Him to rescue me whenever I fall into a pit of sin. That is how I will live with Him today while also looking forward to living with Him in the glories of heaven one day.

T2t: Say no to old and yes to new!

Help **from the Lord:** Pray for God's help to apply your T2t both now and all day long.

> *Father, I do not fully understand this mystery—how Christ crucified my old self on the cross as He also hung there dying all alone and abandoned. And I also cannot completely comprehend how He crushed the power of sin that once held me captive, enslaving my soul. But, by faith, I believe each of these mysterious miracles are true and have been established in my life through my faith in Your Son! Still, it is so easy to lose sight of the reality of what Christ's victory has won for me. I so often lose sight of Your Son when the heat of temptation is on. Instead, help me realize what I'm essentially doing in each moment of weakness. It's as if I am returning to the graveside of my old self to grieve the former life that I lived without You. Open my eyes to see how awful that choice is so that I immediately turn away from all that is old and dead and run toward You and the new life You give me. Enable me to live in the newness You have birthed within me, renewing my mind by removing the old mindset I once clung to as a slave of sin. Go on to awaken my mind to all that is right, honoring, and true through You and Your word. Grab my hand today and every day, dear Father, so that I walk with the One who truly is my Master and Redeemer now and forever. In Jesus' name, amen.*

Yield **to the Lord:** Throughout the day, yield your way for God's way, prayerfully reflecting on how you did at the end of your day.

Week Three Questions for Discussion or Contemplation

Read aloud Day 1, Romans 6:1-3 …

1. How does taking advantage of God's grace by sinning impact your relationship with Him and your own heart (v. 2)?

2. Would any of you be willing to share about one sin you are struggling to die to, and what makes it so hard for you to resist (v. 3)? Or share some examples of sins that are hard for most to resist. What do you think helps strengthen resistance to sin?

3. What are the truths or truth principles we might not have talked about yet from verses 1-3 that catch your attention, and why?

Read aloud Day 2, Romans 6:4-5 …

4. What do you think walking in "newness of life" means and looks like (v. 4)? How are you walking in newness of life?

5. What is your baptism story? Share with us what it meant to you then and how that faith step reflects how you want to live for Christ today.

6. What are the truths or truth principles we might not have talked about yet from verses 4-5 that catch your attention, and why?

Read aloud Day 3, Romans 6:6-8 …

7. What is the difference between "old self" and "sin nature" (v. 6)? If sin has been "brought to nothing," why do you think we still struggle so much with sin?

8. What are some ways we can activate what is true about us through Christ—dying daily to sin (vv. 6-7)?

9. In verse 8, Paul was urging us to focus on when we will live with Christ in eternity. How often do you contemplate this and what do you envision heaven will be like and include?

10. What are the truths or truth principles we might not have talked about yet from verses 6-8 that catch your attention, and why?

11. What is one thing from this past week's study that you want to learn from and live out more?

12. Would anyone like to read a prayer you wrote based on one of the Scriptures from this week? How can we pray for you?

Week Four

10 – Emancipation Proclamation

Week 4, Day 1—Romans 6:9-12

Welcome the Lord!

Open my eyes, that I may behold wondrous things out of your law.
—Psalm 119:18

Observe what the Scripture says:

9 – We know that Christ, being raised from the dead, will never die again; death no longer has dominion over him.
10 – For the death he died he died to sin, once for all, but the life he lives he lives to God.
11 – So you also must consider yourselves dead to sin and alive to God in Christ Jesus.
12 – Let not sin therefore reign in your mortal body, to make you obey its passions.

Recognize what is noteworthy and true:

It's so important to realize how many benefits we, as believers, gain through the death of Christ. And Paul was careful to highlight each one of these in his many letters, saying in verse 9: **"We know that Christ, being raised from the dead, will never die again; death no longer has dominion over him."** The Greek word Paul used for "know" in this verse is "eido" and refers to intuitive knowledge versus experiential knowledge. By using this term, Paul tells us that the Spirit gives us the benefit of knowing certain doctrines and beliefs about Christ, even though we have never witnessed these things or were present to experience them. The Spirit enables us to see and trust that Christ was raised from the dead, will never die again, and is no longer under the control of death. Because Christ is the Mediator and Savior of the redeemed, we benefit from the many victories He has won. For one, we never need to fear death because death no longer holds dominion over us. Once we physically die, we will never die again. And, on the day of our deaths, we will live forever with Jesus in the light of His glory.

In verse 10, Paul added, **"For the death he died he died to sin, once for all, but the life he lives he lives to God."** Christ's death was not simply a physical experience and reality for Him. Jesus' sacrificial death allowed Him to take on and remove the penalty of sin from those He redeems. If not for that victory, humans would remain powerless against sin and, ultimately, condemned to the eternal fires of hell because of our sins. Paul also highlighted how Jesus only had to battle sin and death once. Christ conquered these threats for all who trust in Him and His substitutionary death, burial, and resurrection. Finally, during Jesus' life on earth, He always lived to God, meaning He continually submitted Himself to God the Father for the Father's purposes and will.

Up to this point, Paul focused on what Christ had accomplished and won for our salvation. But now, in verse 11, he turned his focus to what this means for believers, saying, **"So you also must consider yourselves dead to sin and alive to God in Christ Jesus."** Just like Jesus died to sin, believers have also died to sin. And because believers are spiritually alive like Christ, we must also live to God like Jesus did—giving and submitting ourselves to the Father in every possible way.

In verse 12, Paul turned his focus on how believers should and can choose to die to sin, saying, **"Let not sin therefore reign in your mortal body, to make you obey its passions."** We could call this "God's Emancipation Proclamation." Even though we presently remain in our mortal bodies, believers can choose each day not to let sin reign in our hearts or be our master. As long as we live, we will still feel the passions of our sin natures seducing us, tempting us to return to living in sin like we did in our lives before coming to Christ. But, through Christ, we are given the power to resist, not obeying these desires and passions that continue to tempt us day after day. Thankfully, the more we resist these temptations in Christ's power, the more our worldly passions fade into the background, being replaced with more passion for God.

Thought to take:

As believers, we must continually recognize and rejoice over the many benefits we've gained through Christ's death and resurrection. Some of these include no longer needing to fear death and being able to give ourselves fully to God the Father. We dare not take these for granted nor miss the opportunity to apply them daily. Most of all, we owe Christ our lives because of what He paid to redeem us. Just like Jesus died to sin, we too must die to sin, never letting our sinful passions rule over us. Thankfully, Christ already accomplished the hard part—the impossible part—for us. He removed the power and mastery that sin held over us in our former lives, allowing us to walk in freedom—freedom from fear, death, and sin. As I go about this day, I will stop at various points to consider all these many benefits. I will also resist any temptations I face in His strength, continually yielding my heart and giving everything for the One who has set me free.

T2t: Rejoice in Jesus and resist sin

Help from the Lord: Pray for God's help to apply your T2t both now and all day long.

> *Father, how I long to follow Christ and His example by dying to sin, so that I can live closer and give myself more completely to You. Help me realize this doesn't have to be some elusive and unfulfilled desire. I know and trust that Christ has already handed it to me—His victory over what used to hold me captive! Help me consider throughout this day all that Your Son's victory over sin and death means for me. Then use each encouraging truth and reality You bring into focus as a way to deepen my faith in You, enabling me to die to sin and live to You every single day. May I also take these inspiring moments as opportunities to praise and thank You for all You have done and won for me. For it is only in You and Your presence that I find true freedom and joy. So when the heat of temptation is on, when my passions draw me away from my passion for You, give me the strength to resist, returning wholeheartedly to You. Remind me that sin is no longer my master—You are my only Master! Let that be what I demonstrate this and every day, making it evident to all that You are the reigning Lord of my life. You are the One who holds all the power and victory needed to set me free! In Christ's name, amen.*

Yield to the Lord: Throughout the day, yield your way for God's way, prayerfully reflecting on how you did at the end of your day.

11 – 'Altar' Your Life

Week 4, Day 2—Romans 6:13-14

Welcome the Lord!

Open my eyes, that I may behold wondrous things out of your law.
—Psalm 119:18

Observe what the Scripture says:

13 – Do not present your members to sin as instruments for unrighteousness, but present yourselves to God as those who have been brought from death to life, and your members to God as instruments for righteousness.
14 – For sin will have no dominion over you, since you are not under law but under grace.

Recognize what is noteworthy and true:

Living for Christ involves not only knowing what we should do but also what we should not do. Today, we pick up with first part of verse 13: **"Do not present your members to sin as instruments for unrighteousness, …"** where Paul tells us what we are not to do. Here, the word "present" represents how a priest in Old Testament days placed an offering on an altar (Mal. 1:8-13). This particular term and idea would have meant something not only to the Jews in Paul's audience but also to the Gentiles who presented offerings to pagan gods before coming to Christ. In this context, Paul instructs believers not to use the members of our bodies—eyes, ears, lips, hands, feet, mind, etc.—as instruments of anything unrighteous or sinful. The word Paul used for "instruments" here can also be translated as weapons. Ultimately, when we commit unrighteous acts, our bodies become weapons that damage and corrupt ourselves and others.

In the second part of verse 13, Paul spelled out what believers should do, saying, **"but present yourselves to God as those who have been brought from death to life, and your members to God as instruments for righteousness."** Dying to sin by presenting our lives to God mirrors how Jewish priests of old presented sacrifices on the altar. In this exchange, we surrender our desires and purposes for the desires and purposes of God. Paul personalized this sacrifice, making it about our lives, alluding and pointing us to Christ the One who gave His life to redeem the lost. Christ presented the final sacrifice (v. 10) on the altar as our High Priest. Jesus also embodied the sacrifice as the Lamb of God, paying for our sin with His sinless life. Since the redeemed have been brought from life to death through Christ's substitutionary atonement and sacrifice, we owe Him our lives. Therefore, we should never use our lives and bodies as weapons that corrupt or bring discord and dishonor to Christ. Instead, we should not only use but also desire to use our bodies as instruments, playing sweet melodies that bring God glory.

In verse 14, Paul reemphasized the crucial consideration we must keep in place so that we can stand firm each day, saying, **"For sin will have no dominion over you, since you are not under law but under grace."** This verse reminds us of what the redeemed have gained through Christ—freedom from the dominion or reign of sin. Not only should we remember this truth but we should also embrace and live it out every day. God gives us this freedom through His grace, which is separate from the law. God gave the law to us to show us where and how we have gotten off course and sinned, which is a good thing (Rom. 3:20; Gal. 3:18-19). Still, the Mosaic Law is limited because God never designed or intended for the law to save us. Christ's sacrifice enabled Him to replace the Old Covenantal Mosaic Law (a broken and limited system) with the New Covenant based on God's grace. This means that we, as believers, no longer live under the authority of the law nor are condemned by the law. Instead, we live under the authority of God and His grace, where Christ fully equips us with His power to resist every sin and live for Him.

Thought to take:

Paul has thrown down the gauntlet for believers here, challenging us to take stock of at least two essential things regarding our faith. First, how much we trust in the power of Christ's salvation. Second, how much our lives reflect Christ. Are we willingly giving our desires to God daily? Or are we putting the pursuit of earthly pleasures over our pursuit and worship of God? In what ways are we encouraging others to sin? In what ways are we being defensive or remaining in denial about our sinful contribution to the conflicts in our lives? These are just a few of the questions we could prayerfully ask God to answer so that we can repent and resist sin in His power.

We might even want to ask the Lord: How much do I believe Christ has given me the power to resist sin? If we doubt this on any level, then we should ask God to increase our faith in Him and this truth. All of this requires laying, in a spiritual sense, our lives on the altar, making Christ's glory our greatest desire and goal. Since I struggle with this daily, I will start this effort by prayerfully evaluating how much my life reflects Christ. As I go about my day, I will work on strengthening my faith in the Savior's power, resisting sin and giving Him all the glory for each victory.

T2t: Rely on and reflect Christ

Help from the Lord: Pray for God's help to apply your T2t both now and all day long.

> Father, thank You for challenging me to consider how my walk reflects Your Son. Even though this evaluation of my life might be hard or even painful for me to see, I am more than willing to submit myself to Your examination and conviction. So I lay my heart on the altar for You to reveal all the ways I have sinned. Help me see each one. Then help me confess and repent of all the ways I've used my eyes, ears, lips, hands, feet, and mind to pursue unrighteousness. Enable me to feel grieved over all the ways I have come against You and Your good purposes. Allow this exercise to be a turning point for me so that I surrender every part of my life on the altar for You to use as You please. As I go about this day, help me live in Your freedom and grace that empowers me to resist sin and equips me to live out my faith in righteous, good, and Christ-honoring ways. Create opportunities for me to give myself more fully to You today, strengthening my faith each time I obey and follow Your lead. My greatest hope is that these righteous acts will bring Your Son greater glory today and every day. In Jesus' name, amen.

Yield to the Lord: Throughout the day, yield your way for God's way, prayerfully reflecting on how you did at the end of your day.

12 – Fork in the Road

Week 4, Day 3—Romans 6:15-16

Welcome the Lord!

Open my eyes, that I may behold wondrous things out of your law.
—Psalm 119:18

Observe what the Scripture says:

15 – What then? Are we to sin because we are not under law but under grace? By no means!
16 – Do you not know that if you present yourselves to anyone as obedient slaves, you are slaves of the one whom you obey, either of sin, which leads to death, or of obedience, which leads to righteousness?

Recognize what is noteworthy and true:

Since the verse for today begins with a question, we must reflect on the previous Scripture for context. In verses 13-14, Paul communicated the Lord's command to stop presenting ourselves to sin and instead present ourselves to God. Thankfully, Paul takes the time here to explain the "why" behind God's commands, demonstrating the Apostle's love and patience for all he tried to reach and teach.

In verse 15, Paul asked, **"What then? Are we to sin because we are not under law but under grace?"** He then followed that up with this defiant answer, **"By no means!"** This question echoes what Paul posed in verse 1 but with one subtle difference. In verse 1, Paul used a particular Greek word for sin, describing habitual sins and sinful lifestyles. But here he used the Greek term for sin that refers to the occasional failure to obey God and His law. Since believers are no longer under the authority of the law but under grace, we could logically deduce that sinning occasionally is not all that bad—thinking to ourselves, *the grace of God will surely cover it!* But we must put that logic aside, realizing we can never let our guard down when it comes to temptation or sin. God's grace does not give us permission to sin even in the slightest of ways. His grace is what helps us resist sin. Most of all, Christ paid for this grace with His precious blood.

Paul then appealed to these people with a logical argument in verse 16: **"Do you not know that if you present yourselves to anyone as obedient slaves, you are slaves of the one whom you obey, either of sin, which leads to death, or of obedience, which leads to righteousness?"** Paul wasn't really questioning whether these people knew this truth. He wanted them and us to take the opportunity to think about how this truth plays out in our lives. We only have two choices—either to sin or to obey God. There really is no third, neutral option. We cannot simply stand on the sidelines of life and do nothing, believing the grace of God covers our inaction. Inaction is actually passive disobedience. Paul then strategically posed the idea of people presenting themselves as obedient slaves to two different masters. The first master represents "sin" and the second represents "obedience" (to God). The sentence structure in Greek uses the word "present" in a way that highlights our willingness to give ourselves as slaves to one or the other master. God gives believers the power to willingly obey Him over willingly obeying sin. The same is not true for unbelievers since they are operating apart from Christ. This ultimately means unbelievers resist the power and freedom found in Christ. Paul highlighted the distinction of this choice when he cast it between choosing sin and death or choosing obedience and righteousness. As believers—freed from the dominion of sin—we have the glad choice and limitless power to choose obedience. When we make this choice, we progress in our righteousness (sanctification), ultimately, reflecting and honoring God.

Thought to take:

Throughout our day, we face multiple forks in the road—junctures where we must choose to obey sin or to obey God. We cannot stand at the fork and do nothing since this too is a choice to disobey God. We also cannot assume that subtle, smaller, or occasional sins are any less destructive to our lives than larger, willful sins. As believers, our sins might not lead to eternal death and destruction like they do for unbelievers, but they are also extremely dangerous and destructive to our and other people's spiritual health. With these realities and truths in mind, I will strive to present my life and choices on the altar to God today, willingly resisting sin and obeying Christ through His power rather than in my own strength.

T2t: Rely on God's grace to obey

Help **from the Lord:** Pray for God's help to apply your T2t both now and all day long.

Father, Your grace is so rich, deep, and unconditional that I often feel tempted to take it for granted. That is why I must take this warning and command very seriously. I should not focus on how You do not reject me because of Your grace. Instead, I should remember that my sin severely weakens my faith in You, pulling me away from You and Your will. So help me understand just how precious Your grace is. Remind me of how much it cost Jesus to provide this life-transforming gift. Go further, reminding me of how costly it is to myself and others when I don't rely on You. How it represents a choice to go backward toward my former life, down destructive paths, even when I sin in the slightest of ways. As I lay my heart on the altar, keep it soft and tender toward You and Your will so I can resist every temptation that inevitably will emerge in my path with Your strength. For I know that I cannot escape the choice to sin by doing nothing. With each choice that comes along, I must act in faith. I must walk out my reliance on You, going in Your direction and always choosing You over myself. For, You are my Master; and that's where I want my heart to stay, bowing willingly at Your feet. I give all of myself to You for You and Your good purposes to be done in my life. In Jesus' name, amen.

Yield **to the Lord:** Throughout the day, yield your way for God's way, prayerfully reflecting on how you did at the end of your day.

Week Four Questions for Discussion or Contemplation

Read aloud Day 1, Romans 6:9-12 ...

1. Why do you think Paul emphasized how Jesus only had to die once to sin (vv. 9-10)?

2. Why do you think God enables believers to "know" (Gr. "eido") certain doctrines and beliefs about Christ, even though we have not witnessed or experienced them firsthand (v. 9)?

3. When believers face temptation, what are some things we can do to strengthen our resolve to avoid letting sin reign in our mortal bodies (v. 12)?

4. What are the truths or truth principles we might not have talked about yet from verses 9-12 that catch your attention, and why?

Read aloud Day 2, Romans 6:13-14 ...

5. What are some common temptations for believers that involve using our "eyes" as instruments (weapons) of unrighteousness (v. 13)? Lips? Hands? What are some ways to use our "members" as instruments that play sweet melodies for God's glory?

6. What are some meaningful, even creative, ways to "present" a sin offering to God, mirroring how the priests presented offerings (v. 13)?

7. What are the truths or truth principles we might not have talked about yet from verses 13-14 that catch your attention, and why?

Read aloud Day 3, Romans 6:15-16 ...

8. Describe a time when you compared your sins to someone else's, thinking I would never do something that bad. In light of verses 15 and 16, what if your sin is less serious—what are the implications of letting your mind focus on that disparity? What is ultimately true?

9. What are the truths or truth principles we might not have talked about yet from verses 15-16 that catch your attention, and why?

10. What is one thing from this past week's study that you want to learn from and live out more?

11. Would anyone like to read a prayer you wrote based on one of the Scriptures from this week? How can we pray for you?

Week Five

13 - Free Hearts

Week 5, Day 1—Romans 6:17-19a

Welcome the Lord!

Open my eyes, that I may behold wondrous things out of your law.
—Psalm 119:18

Observe what the Scripture says:

17 – But thanks be to God, that you who were once slaves of sin have become obedient from the heart to the standard of teaching to which you
were committed,
18 – and, having been set free from sin, have become slaves of righteousness.
19a – I am speaking in human terms, because of your natural limitations.

Recognize what is noteworthy and true:

Paul shifted his focus in today's reading, signaling a contrast from his previous message with one simple word, **"But . . ."** while continuing with, **"thanks be to God, that you who were once slaves of sin have become obedient from the heart . . ."** (v. 17). Paul spoke directly to the redeemed in this Roman church since they were "once slaves of sin" and now were living "obedient from the heart." Highlighting obedience from the heart points out that these believers were not just guided by head knowledge but also were seeking and obeying God from their core—from their new, redeemed hearts (v. 4). Paul's thankfulness that these believers were living obediently is linked to what he said in verse 16 about believers choosing to disobey God. He could now rejoice because these believers were choosing to obey rather than disobey.

Paul continued on with what these believers were **"committed"** to, saying, **"to the standard of teaching . . ."** (v. 17). The Greek word Paul used for "standard" here relates to a mold or pattern. In Paul's day, artisans pressed clay or wax into this kind of mold, transforming the substance into a desired shape. The Greek word Paul used for "committed" captures the idea of believers willingly handing our lives over to God. Like in verse 16, believers are to commit ourselves to God, allowing Him, as our Master, to form us into whatever shape He desires and use us in whatever way He decides is best. We surrender ourselves to God's standard through repeatedly listening and obeying teaching (doctrine) that accurately declares the gospel. Everything we think, feel, and do must flow from the standard of teaching reflected in the gospel.

In verse 18, Paul illustrates the outcome of obeying from the heart and committing ourselves to the gospel: **"and, having been set free from sin, have become slaves of righteousness."** As the redeemed, we are not just set free from sin but, in the exchange, become slaves of righteousness. This phraseology—moving from slaves of sin to slaves of righteousness and Christ—might have rattled these Roman believers who feared slavery. However, it is one of many beautiful mysteries and paradoxes of God. When we receive Christ's salvation, we are set free to be His slaves, where freedoms and joys abound through His lavish grace and love. As slaves of righteousness, God enables us to live in the righteousness of Christ, consistently demonstrating godly attitudes and conduct like our Savior.

In verse 19a, Paul gave a caveat to this comparison, **"I am speaking in human terms, because of your natural limitations."** At this time in history, the Roman church probably was comprised of both free citizens and slaves, making this comparison very unpleasant just like it is for us today. Yet because of our limited human understanding, Paul offered the closest concept and comparison for illustrating how much believers belong to and should be devoted to God, challenging us to adopt a positive view of slavery to righteousness.

Thought to take:

In the passage for today, Paul strongly emphasized the need for believers to obey God from the heart—to give ourselves completely to Him and His righteous will. This reality should not feel like a robbery with our hands stuck up high in the air. It should feel like we are handing over our hearts to the One we know will treat us with the utmost love and care (Jn. 15:15). If any of us doubts this or doesn't know how to trust God in this way, the way forward is to engage our faith and commit ourselves to living out the gospel. When we do, we will experience the reliability, wisdom, and encouragement found in the teaching of Christ. We will gladly declare ourselves slaves of Christ because, as we live out His right ways, we will experience the greatest freedom and joy possible. I will take up this challenge, renewing my commitment to live out the gospel while also holding out my whole heart for Jesus to keep safe and guide. I will rest in His powerful hands while He enables me to resist temptation and do what is right and good at every turn in my day.

T2t: Keep my heart in Jesus' hands

Help from the Lord: Pray for God's help to apply your T2t both now and all day long.

> *Father, when I was a slave to sin, I could not see or even imagine all the freedoms and joys that come from handing my heart over to You. For, You could have left me in that blind and enslaved state, yet You made me one of Your own! How amazing is that?! I thank You for opening my eyes to the gospel and inviting me to be both Your slave of righteousness and Your beloved child—kept secure in the warm, affectionate bond of Your love! Thank You for not only removing the chains of sin from my life but also offering me the robe of Christ's righteousness to wear. A robe bought with Your Son's precious blood. Now all I want to do is live out the gospel—to spread the good news to all who will listen to my testimony, seeing my yielded life on display for Your glory. Allow as many as possible to see our loving bond through my attitude and actions today and every day. Use my secure relationship with You to draw them to You—the One who can also free them from their sin and give them the best life ever! Empower me to live out Your right and good ways this day and I will rejoice in the freedoms and joys I experience through the surrendered life. In Christ's name, amen.*

Yield to the Lord: Throughout the day, yield your way for God's way, prayerfully reflecting on how you did at the end of your day.

14 – Good Fruit

Week 5, Day 2—Romans 6:19b-21a

Welcome the Lord!

Open my eyes, that I may behold wondrous things out of your law.
—Psalm 119:18

Observe what the Scripture says:

19b – For just as you once presented your members as slaves to impurity and to lawlessness leading to more lawlessness, so now present your members as slaves to righteousness leading to sanctification.
20 – For when you were slaves of sin, you were free in regard to righteousness.
21a – But what fruit were you getting at that time from the things of which you are now ashamed?

Recognize what is noteworthy and true:

Paul continued to urge these believers to understand the spiritual relationship that is always in play for us, making it impossible for us to remain spiritually neutral. Starting off in verse 19b, Paul said, **"For just as you once presented your members as slaves to impurity and to lawlessness leading to more lawlessness, so now present your members as slaves to righteousness leading to sanctification."** Paul personified two slave masters, calling them "lawlessness" and "righteousness" to help us understand the significance between our choice to sin and choice to obey. As we make choices, we often are not fully aware of how much or whether we are submitting to one or the other of these. Yet we must never underestimate the power our choices make in defining our allegiances. "Forks in the road" are a constant in the spiritual battles of life, requiring us to choose between one or the other of these two masters.

The Greek word Paul used in verse 19b for "presented" was written in the Greek aorist tense. This inflection emphasizes how we, who wholeheartedly presented ourselves as slaves of impurity, sin, and lawlessness in the past, must instead wholeheartedly present ourselves as slaves to righteousness now. Paul also emphasized how slavery to impurity (sin) leads to lawlessness, allowing lawlessness to take over more and more of our hearts. The term lawlessness means having no law (moral law) to obey or follow, living as if you are the one in charge. You feel as if you can call all the shots instead of trusting your choices and life to God. Thankfully, presenting ourselves to righteousness also leads to something more— "sanctification." The word sanctification means "to be set apart" (for God's use) and involves a moment-by-moment process of choosing to obey God. We do not automatically or quickly receive sanctification from God like we do righteousness, which is something God grants immediately when we place our faith in Christ. Sanctification is a process of working out our salvation and results in progressive growth toward spiritual maturity (Phil. 2:12).

In verse 20, Paul further clarified this doctrinal principle when he said, **"For when you were slaves of sin, you were free in regard to righteousness."** While we were still slaves to sin, we possessed a brand of freedom—a freedom from righteousness and the law (5:13). Before receiving salvation, sin dominated our minds, trying to convince us that living in Christ's righteousness is both undesirable and too restrictive for us. We might have felt free to choose our own way when enslaved to sin, but we could not see or realize just how terrible the taskmaster of sin was and is. We could not see how truly free our enslavement to Christ makes us as we rest now in His bond of love and walk in His spacious paths of freedom.

In verse 21a, Paul brought these sinful choices into perspective when he said, **"But what fruit were you getting at that time from the things of which you are now ashamed?"** Lawlessness produces more and more sinful fruit (sins that take root, grow, spread, and multiply exponentially), not to mention adding the burden of shame to our lives. The phrase "at that time" allowed Paul to highlight how a Christ-follower feels now about sin whenever we recognize it through the conviction of the Holy Spirit. Believers should feel a healthy sense of shame (guilt, not condemnation) about any sinful lifestyle we were or are living. God uses that sense of conviction to point us back to repentance and right (righteous) choices where Christ waits, ready to lift this burden from our shoulders.

Thought to take:

Two main takeaways are catching my eye from this reading. First, we are either all in with sin or all in with God. Being half-hearted in our faith reflects the choice to resist Christ. Second, we produce more and more of what we pursue and cultivate during our lifetimes—whether that's good fruit or bad. Thankfully, God has done the hardest work—impossible, really—for Christ-followers by providing our salvation and righteousness through His death. But I'm also thankful that God offers us the opportunity to cooperate and work with Him in the sanctification process by resisting sin and committing ourselves to Christ- and gospel-centered living. What choices are you and I making that grow and produce good spiritual fruit on any given day? My goal today will be to give myself wholeheartedly to God, growing in my faith by resisting sin, and producing good spiritual fruit for His power.

T2t: Do what produces "good fruit"

Help from the Lord: Pray for God's help to apply your T2t both now and all day long.

> Father, I am so grateful that You have extended the opportunity for me to join You in the pursuit and process of spiritual growth—to become more like Christ. Because I know that You did not save me so that I could stand idly by on the sidelines of life, enjoying the many blessings of Your grace and righteousness while producing nothing for You. Looking at my life, I see so many areas where I need to grow, even corners of my life where I am barren. I desperately need to send down deeper roots into the truths and power of the gospel, so that I can produce fruit for You. If I do not present my eyes, ears, lips, and life more consistently and completely to You and Your righteous ways, my fruitfulness for You will suffer. So help me seize every opportunity You give me. May I present myself to You like a gift wrapped in Your glory and grace for everyone to open up and receive. Remind me in moments of temptation to resist sins, knowing each choice to disobey can easily lead to more and more sinfulness and hardheartedness. Energize me for the honorable task of working out my salvation today, allowing my faith and sanctification to grow deeper still. Enable others to see the difference You have made in my life, tasting the good fruit You produce through me. Use this to convince them that You are my Master and greatest Love so that \\\\\they too will chase after Your love! In Jesus' name, amen.

Yield to the Lord: Throughout the day, yield your way for God's way, prayerfully reflecting on how you did at the end of your day.

15 – The Christ-follower's Comma

Week 5, Day 3—Romans 6:21b-23

Welcome the Lord!

> Open my eyes, that I may behold wondrous things out of your law.
> —Psalm 119:18

Observe what the Scripture says:

21b – For the end of those things is death.
22 – But now that you have been set free from sin and have become slaves of God, the fruit you get leads to sanctification and its end, eternal life.
23 – For the wages of sin is death, but the free gift of God is eternal life in Christ Jesus our Lord.

Recognize what is noteworthy and true:

In today's reading, Paul referred to the former sinful lifestyles of Christ-followers with the question he asked in verse 21a, "But what fruit were you getting at that time from the things of which you are now ashamed?" He then named this fruit in 21b, never soft-pedaling what results from pursuing a sinful lifestyle: **"For the end of those things is death."** The Greek word Paul used for "end" not only points to a stopping point but also includes the idea of culminating in a goal. Ultimately, "death" comes (culminates) when we continue to choose sin over obeying God. The word Paul used for "death" here refers to both our physical deaths and the quality of our lives whenever we choose sin over obedience to God (1 Tim. 5:6). We might think that dying to Christ is worse or harder than indulging in sin but the damage our sins do to the quality of our lives and relationships tells another story.

In verse 22, Paul added, **"But now that you have been set free from sin and have become slaves of God, the fruit you get leads to sanctification and its end, eternal life."** When we sin, we produce bad fruit. But when Christ-followers resist sin and obey God, we produce good spiritual fruit (Gal.5:22-23). Not only does this good spiritual fruit produce sanctification—deepening our faith, spiritual growth, and purity—but the ultimate fruit of our salvation is "eternal life." Some think that eternal life begins when we die. But for believers—made alive in Christ (Eph. 2:4-5)—our eternal lives begin the day we receive salvation. Think of it this way, the physical death of a believer figuratively represents a comma rather than a period. Eternal life offers us the most abundant life possible here on earth and also assures us the never-ending glories and joys of being with Jesus in heaven one day.

In verse 23, Paul proclaimed one of the most iconic and foundational truths of the gospel when he said, **"For the wages of sin is death, but the free gift of God is eternal life in Christ Jesus our Lord."** There is a common pattern in Scripture that shows God first offering the bad news that might crush our spirits before exalting us to the heights with His too-good-to-be-true good news. The bad news here is that we owe wages to God for the sins we commit. The Greek word "wages" comes from a military term, describing a soldier's rations. Paul likely used this term to reinforce the military theme he had spoken of earlier when he used the word "instruments," meaning weapons (Rom. 6:13), reminding us we are in a spiritual war. Thankfully, through Christ's victory, we are empowered to fight as victors over sin in this war every single day. Paul then juxtaposed the phrase "wages of sin" with "free gift of God" to magnify what Christ has done and won for us. Christ paid the debt of sin we owed—a debt we could never afford to repay to God. In paying our debt, Christ freed us from the wages of sin and death, giving us eternal life to boot. Paul intentionally referred to Christ as "Lord" here as a way to reemphasize Jesus' position as the believer's Lord and Master. He is the One who has captured our hearts with the free gift bought with His grace.

Thought to take:

There are so many implications and applications we could identify from this passage. Far too many for me to go into here. But I will offer just a few to stimulate your thinking. For those who are trying to work for their salvation, they must recognize they owe God far more than they could ever repay on their own. These individuals need to receive the gift of eternal life, through Christ, knowing He is the only One who could pay the highest price to provide salvation. For believers, I can think of at least two ways to apply a "Thought to take." The first is to recognize the need to resist sin with God's power. We must remember how it destroys and damages our lives in so many ways, while obeying our Master produces good spiritual fruit. Another thought we could take focuses on the gift of eternal life. As a believer, I can rejoice in the abundant eternal life I am experiencing today, and thank God for the never-ending life I will experience in eternity one day. Both realities will encourage me in the challenges of this day.

T2t: Resist sin; Rejoice over eternal life

Help from the Lord: Pray for God's help to apply your T2t both now and all day long.

> *Father, You have made knowing how to experience a saving and unhindered relationship with You so very clear through Paul's words here today. Yet I see so many in life who are trying feverishly and pointlessly to earn what only Christ could provide and pay. Open their eyes to see You offering them this free gift! I also want to thank You for opening my eyes to Your gospel truth, enabling me to receive this gift, paid for and free through Christ's grace and goodness. For, I know there was nothing good in me to draw You to me. Yet because You are the personification of Love, You saved me, setting me apart for Your service. Enable me to realize just how privileged and blessed it is to be Your slave—a slave who enjoys greater freedoms and more abundance than the richest and most powerful of this world. Help me realize and see the damage my sins can do to my life and relationships. Your gift through Christ has ultimately removed the sting of death from my life, but not the corrosive consequences that hinder my spiritual growth and tarnish my testimony. With that in mind, empower me today and every day to pursue Your will, living yielded to You and Your gospel. Use every act of devotion I do in Your name to deepen my spiritual growth. As I stoop to serve others, remind me of how Christ plumbed the depths of service, sacrifice, and surrender for me as well. Thank You that Christ is my Master and went before me in humility to win the victory over sin and death. In Jesus' name, amen.*

Yield to the Lord: Throughout the day, yield your way for God's way, prayerfully reflecting on how you did at the end of your day.

Week Five Questions for Discussion or Contemplation

Read aloud Day 1, Romans 6:17-19a ...

1. How can we know or determine whether we are being obedient to God "from the heart" (v. 17)?

2. What are some ways you are committed to "molding" yourself more into Christ's likeness (v. 17)?

3. As a believer, how do you feel about being urged to accept and pursue the title of "slave of righteousness" (v. 18)?

4. Why do you think the phrase "slaves of righteousness" is one of the best ways to describe the believer's commitment to Christ (v. 18)?

5. What are the truths or truth principles we might not have talked about yet from verses 17-19a that catch your attention, and why?

Read aloud Days 2 and 3, Romans 6:19b-23 ...

6. Think of an unresolved conflict or disappointment in your life. What are some of the bad choices you've made in your attitude or actions, producing more of the same in your situation (v. 19b)?

7. What can you do to turn your focus toward "righteousness"?

8. How can you discern between feeling ashamed because of God's conviction and feeling condemned (v. 21)? Regarding this issue, what types of thoughts lead to life? Lead to death?

9. How can we improve on the amount of good spiritual fruit we produce (v. 22)? What is one good spiritual "fruit" (Gal. 5:22-23 for examples) that you want to produce more of in your life, and why?

10. What are the truths or truth principles we might not have talked about yet from verses 19b-23 that catch your attention, and why?

11. What is one thing from this past week's study that you want to learn from and live out more?

12. Would anyone like to read a prayer you wrote based on one of the Scriptures from this week? How can we pray for you?

Week Six

16 – Who are You Devoted to?

Week 6, Day 1—Romans 7:1-3

Welcome the Lord!

Open my eyes, that I may behold wondrous things out of your law.
—Psalm 119:18

Observe what the Scripture says:

1 – Or do you not know, brothers—for I am speaking to those who know the law—that the law is binding on a person only as long as he lives?
2 – For a married woman is bound by law to her husband while he lives, but if her husband dies she is released from the law of marriage.
3 – Accordingly, she will be called an adulteress if she lives with another man while her husband is alive. But if her husband dies, she is free from that law, and if she marries another man she is not an adulteress.

Recognize what is noteworthy and true:

Almost without taking a breath, Paul moved from discussing grace in chapter 6 to matters related to the law in chapter 7. Some in this church did not understand how being "under grace" altered their relationship to the law. Naturally, Paul wanted to address their haziness on this in verse 1: **"Or do you not know, brothers—for I am speaking to those who know the law—that the law is binding on a person only as long as he lives?"** The wording in the Greek manuscript does not include the article "the" before "law" in this verse, indicating Paul was referring to general societal laws and not specifically to the Mosaic Law to illustrate his point. This rhetorical question assumes that everyone agrees with the idea that as long as we live on earth, we are bound and expected to obey the law.

In verse 2, Paul offered a real-life metaphor for illustrating how the law operates, saying, **"For a married woman is bound by law to her husband while he lives, but if her husband dies she is released from the law of marriage."** Paul was not trying to discuss the importance of keeping the marriage covenant here, although that is necessary and true. He wanted to reflect upon something these people knew quite a bit about—how the Mosaic Law worked in cases of divorce. They knew the Mosaic Law did not permit a wife to remarry until after the death of her husband. This scenario helped Paul show how the law binds us to certain choices and relationships. It also illustrates how death releases us from the requirements of the law. Lastly, it highlights how Christ's death frees the believer, in a spiritual sense, from the dominion of the law. Through Christ's death, we are free to resist sin, choosing obedience and life instead of rebellion and death.

In verse 3, Paul discussed one severe consequence wives experienced for disobeying this law: **"Accordingly, she will be called an adulteress if she lives with another man while her husband is alive. But if her husband dies, she is free from that law, and if she marries another man she is not an adulteress."** Paul used this physical and relational reality to illustrate a spiritual one. In both Old and New Testament days, whenever a woman divorced her husband so that she could marry another man, she was called an adulteress. Jews would have viewed her as someone who chose to be unfaithful to her husband by breaking this law. However, if she waited until after her husband died, this Mosaic law no longer applied to her situation, freeing her to marry again. In a similar way, believers have died to the law through Christ, freeing us to marry and belong to Him as His bride.

Thought to take:

Some in this church were leaning far too heavily on the law to gain God's acceptance. They were not making the connection between Christ's death and how that cleared the path for a new relationship with Him. Even after you and I give our lives to Jesus, it is easy to do the same. We can stay locked in a union of sorts with the law and legalism rather than embracing the new union we have with Jesus through our faith in Him. Paul's words here today remind me to leave my old life behind. To quit trying to prove my righteousness to God since trying to earn "my righteousness without Christ" is like having an affair with the Law. Trying to keep the law without anchoring my life in Christ actually results in feeling ashamed and distant from Him. So today, I will thank Jesus for dying for and releasing me from the tyranny of the law through His grace. I will also rest and rely on His power and salvation that enables me to remain devoted to Him alone.

T2t: Rest in and rely on Jesus

Help from the Lord: Pray for God's help to apply your T2t both now and all day long.

> *Jesus, I am so grateful You found a way to break the bond and power that the Law held over my life. Never let me fall prey again to the lie that following Your Law can provide what I need to be accepted by You. For, I am convinced now that You and Your grace are all I need for my salvation! Your grace is all I need to be accepted as Your bride. It wasn't long ago that I was married to the most tyrannical spouse ever—"the law." But since coming to faith in You, I have died to the law, which allows me to enjoy my new life and unfettered union with You, my beautiful Bridegroom. Without Your saving grace, all that the law did for me was leave me shackled in my sins, facing death and certain destruction in eternity. But now You give me freedom to live for You through my dependence on Your salvation, power, and love. May I never rely on my own efforts to win Your heart again. Instead, empower me to choose You each day so that I remain dependent on You when everything within me screams for independence and faulty self-reliance. Thank You for Your love that is the only perfectly true and faithful love in all of life. In Your name, amen.*

Yield to the Lord: Throughout the day, yield your way for God's way, prayerfully reflecting on how you did at the end of your day.

17 – New Source and Way

Week 6, Day 2—Romans 7:4-6

Welcome the Lord!

Open my eyes, that I may behold wondrous things out of your law.
—Psalm 119:18

Observe what the Scripture says:

4 – Likewise, my brothers, you also have died to the law through the body of Christ, so that you may belong to another, to him who has been raised from the dead, in order that we may bear fruit for God.
5 – For while we were living in the flesh, our sinful passions, aroused by the law, were at work in our members to bear fruit for death.
6 – But now we are released from the law, having died to that which held us captive, so that we serve in the new way of the Spirit and not in the old way of the written code.

Recognize what is noteworthy and true:

Up to this point, Paul had already established how believers have died to sin. But beginning here in verse 4, he unveiled what death to sin means for the redeemed: **"Likewise, my brothers, you also have died to the law through the body of Christ, so that you may belong to another, to him who has been raised from the dead, in order that we may bear fruit for God."** Notice that Christ-followers have died to the law through Christ's body and death (6:5) and not that the law has died or is no longer useful. Christ's death and resurrection allow believers to "belong to another"—to, in a spiritual sense, marry Him, our ultimate Bridegroom. Unbelievers must realize that they can never justify themselves before God through their flawed and imperfect attempts to obey the law. And as believers, we must rely on the Spirit at all times instead of relying on ourselves and trying in our human strength to obey God. The believer's covenant and union are with Jesus—the only true Source of power that enables us to keep God's law and bear spiritual fruit.

For the sake of comparison, Paul refocused on the old and unredeemed lives of believers in verse 5: **"For while we were living in the flesh, our sinful passions, aroused by the law, were at work in our members to bear fruit for death."** The Greek word for "flesh" here is "sarx" and includes many nuanced ideas and applications related to the sin nature. In this context, it generally refers to how we lived immorally before coming to Christ. During that time, we continually sought to gratify our selfish and sinful passions rather than pursuing God. While we were living in the flesh, our sin natures were "aroused" by the law, tempted to sin even more, bearing fruit for death. Our renegade passions and sin nature were the problem—not the law. Ironically, when the law is in human hands, it makes sin seem more appealing than doing good or obeying God. Sin becomes the "forbidden fruit" —tantalizingly out of reach and seductively dangerous to us. Not surprisingly, whenever we take and consume this forbidden fruit, it leaves believers with a spiritual bellyache (at the very least). Worse still, it is deadly for the unbeliever, resulting in death in eternity and spiritual deadness to God's truth.

In verse 6, Paul went on to share good news coming from the bad with these encouraging words, **"But now we are released from the law, having died to that which held us captive, so that we serve in the new way of the Spirit and not in the old way of the written code."** Christ-followers are released from the captivity and condemnation of the law, arising from our sinful nature and futile attempts to gain justification through the law. Believers are servants, living out the "new way" as the Spirit governs and directs us from within. Since Christ's victory over death and sin, God has written His law on the hearts of the redeemed rather than leaving it simply as the written code detached from us on the pages of our Bibles (Rom. 2:12-16).

Thought to take:

When I was a young child, I placed my faith in Christ. Because of that defining decision and faith step, I don't think I've ever knowingly tried to earn my salvation by following the law of God. I was just far too young and simple at that time to think that I could accomplish such a huge feat on my own or even see the necessity for it. Still, as an adult believer, I can easily give in to a version of this kind of thinking, seeking to accomplish feats that only Christ can do through the Spirit within me. In the day-to-day struggles of life, I constantly need the Spirit to remind me to resist temptations in Christ's power rather than in my own strength and understanding. God also uses my studies in and application of Scripture along with prayer every day to guide and empower me to bear fruit for Him. Because of that, I will take what I've studied here and seek to live out these truths in the power of the Spirit rather than in my own strength.

T2t: Look to the Spirit for truth and power

Help **from the Lord:** Pray for God's help to apply your T2t both now and all day long.

> *Father, I'm so grateful that You could see, anticipate, and know how I would abuse Your good and helpful Law. Amazingly, You went even further, giving me the only sacrifice and solution for this problem—Your Son's pure life for my sinful one. Thank You for raising my dead spirit to new life, going further to fill me with Your Spirit while also empowering me for every challenge I encounter. What an intimate and multi-faceted gift! What a joyful reality, knowing You are with me every step of the way, guiding and enabling me to do Your will in the confines of my heart and beyond. You accept me, not because I faithfully follow the Mosaic Law or do enough good works to achieve some elusive standard. I do thank You for Your law and the Scriptures since they are welcome reminders of how to live out Your will. But I also know they cannot save me. All I must do is rely on the redemptive work Your Spirit has already done in my heart because of my faith in Christ. Then and only then can I cooperate with You, growing stronger in my faith as I obey Your word, laws, and Spirit each day. When I'm enticed to sin today—when my sinful nature is aroused within me—open my eyes to see what is truly happening. In the tension of being pulled toward sin, pull me closer to You, empowering me to resist sin in Your power. Allow me to remain fully devoted to You, the only Source for life, godliness, and salvation. In Christ's name, amen.*

Yield **to the Lord:** Throughout the day, yield your way for God's way, prayerfully reflecting on how you did at the end of your day.

18 – X-Ray Vision

Week 6, Day 3—Romans 7:7-8

Welcome the Lord!

Open my eyes, that I may behold wondrous things out of your law.
—Psalm 119:18

Observe what the Scripture says:

7 – What then shall we say? That the law is sin? By no means! Yet if it had not been for the law, I would not have known sin. For I would not have known what it is to covet if the law had not said, "You shall not covet."
8 – But sin, seizing an opportunity through the commandment, produced in me all kinds of covetousness. For apart from the law, sin lies dead.

Recognize what is noteworthy and true:

Previously, Paul had established how believers are not under the authority of the law but rather under the authority of God and His "grace" (6:15). Yet, in verse 7, he focused on how believers might foolishly put themselves under the law, asking these questions to stir greater understanding of this principle: **"What then shall we say? That the law is sin?"** Paul knew that some legalistic Jews among this flock would likely object to this teaching. And he also realized that this new way of thinking about the law might be equated with sin since he declared that being aware of God's law arouses sin. If that was what they assumed about this message, Paul was here to tell them their line of thinking was patently false.

In the latter part of verse 7, Paul explained why, exclaiming, **"By no means! Yet if it had not been for the law, I would not have known sin. For I would not have known what it is to covet if the law had not said, 'You shall not** covet.'" Paul boldly debunked such thinking, further clarifying why God gave us the law in the first place. Without the law guiding our choices and opening our eyes to the truth, we would never know when we are choosing to sin. We would never know that coveting is wrong without the law pointing out to us this particular sin (Ex. 20:17) or any other sins. This means we can remain oblivious and in denial to the fact that we are coveting or committing any other sin. As for coveting, without the law convicting us, we can easily justify that our thoughts are right (righteous) when we are actually sinning. Thankfully, the law operates like an X-ray, showing us where the problem is. We would never blame the X-ray or X-ray technician for discovering a broken bone or cancer when it's revealed on the film. We would be thankful the X-ray identified the problem. However, the X-ray does not correct the issue—only brings it to light so the physician can.

In verse 8, Paul reiterated how the sin nature operates when the law comes into play, saying, **"But sin, seizing an opportunity through the commandment, produced in me all kinds of covetousness. For apart from the law, sin lies dead."** We all know that saying "no" to an independent toddler or a rebellious teenager is like dangling a carrot before a hungry horse. Being told no prompts them to race toward it faster when not hungry than when they are unaware of the carrot and starving. It's the same for all of us no matter our age. Because of our awareness of God's commands, our sin nature entices us to live independent of the law, rebelling against it because God says "no" to certain choices. Paul likely picked the sin of "covetousness" to illustrate this point because it is at the heart of many other types of sin. It is a desire for something more or something different than what we have, causing us to question God's goodness and provision. Paul concluded this verse with the truth that apart from the law our desire to sin would remain dormant or "dead." This outcome highlights how our sin nature perverts our perspective about the law, deadening us to how helpful it can be for our spiritual growth and understanding of God.

Thought to take:

Today's passage exposes two reasons why humans often resist the gospel and gospel-empowered living. First, we can be like some in this church, still clinging to the belief that obeying God's law can win His favor and earn justification. No one has the power, sinlessness, or willingness to do that for us—other than Christ! Second, we can foolishly view the law of God as something far too restrictive or unfair, rebelling against it by pursuing our own human desires. We might not even be aware of this movement away from Christ. This is just one reason why we desperately need the law of God and Spirit to guide and correct us. We resolve this resistance by humbly submitting to God's gospel and law, relying on the indwelling Spirit to live out our faith every day of our lives. This will be what I focus on and strive for today. I will choose to submit to God and His gospel truth, including accepting every no or yes that He asks me to embrace, honor, and do.

T2t: Submit to God's "nos" and "yeses"

Help from the Lord: Pray for God's help to apply your T2t both now and all day long.

> *Father, as the old psalm goes, Your "boundary lines have fallen for me in pleasant places" (Ps. 16:5a). And I'm so thankful that I feel this way about Your boundaries now, although I can only truly see it this way because of Your Spirit's indwelling. Now, when I feel tempted to sin, Your Spirit helps right my wrong perspective, whispering the truth and wisdom of Your word in my ear. I implore You to keep lighting my path and opening my eyes and ears to all of Your "nos and yeses" as I go along the way each day. Whenever I encounter one today, move me to embrace and live it out with actions that honor You. Keep me from falling for the lie that I can achieve anything of worth in my own weak, human power. And reveal the even more seductive lie, telling me that my sinful desires are where I can find satisfaction and meaning in life. Instead, use Your law and truth to convince me to obey so that I yield to You and Your word when the heat is on. Pour on Your power, Lord, because I know how truly weak and limited my strength is! I cannot be humble or submit to You without Your Spirit convicting and energizing me to act in good and right ways. I give myself wholeheartedly to living out the gospel and Your Law today, knowing You will use my kind and righteous acts to inspire, compel, and draw others to You and Your good news. In Christ's name, amen.*

Yield to the Lord: Throughout the day, yield your way for God's way, prayerfully reflecting on how you did at the end of your day.

Week Six Questions for Discussion or Contemplation

Read aloud Day 1, Romans 7:1-3 …

1. What are some of the typical things unbelievers think they can do to try to earn salvation? Where do people get these ideas?

2. What implications emerge from the spiritual truth and reality that the law no longer is binding on a believer (v. 1)?

3. Why do you think Paul used the metaphor of an adulteress to illustrate "spiritual adultery" (v. 3)?

4. What are the truths or truth principles we might not have talked about yet from verses 1-3 that catch your attention, and why?

Read aloud Day 2, Romans 7:4-6 …

5. When have you recently felt God impressing on your heart to do some good action—to bear spiritual fruit (v. 4), and what was it? How can you know that your impression is from God?

6. What do you think Paul meant when he said we are "aroused by the law" to sin (v. 5)? Why do you think God wants it to work this way?

7. What are the truths or truth principles we might not have talked about yet from verses 4-6 that catch your attention, and why?

Read aloud Day 3, Romans 7:7-8 …

8. Describe a time when God's word convicted you, revealing a sin that you didn't even know you were committing (v. 7)? How did you feel and what did you do after becoming aware of your sin?

9. If "apart from the law, sin lies dead" (we aren't as tempted to sin), why doesn't God just remove the law from our lives (v. 8)?

10. What are some good things the law has corrected in your life?

11. What are the truths or truth principles we might not have talked about yet from verses 7-8 that catch your attention, and why?

12. What is one thing from this past week's study that you want to learn from and live out more?

13. Would anyone like to read a prayer you wrote based on one of the Scriptures from this week? How can we pray for you?

Week Seven

19 – The 'Silent Killer'

Week 7, Day 1—Romans 7:9-12

Welcome the Lord!

Open my eyes, that I may behold wondrous things out of your law.
—Psalm 119:18

Observe what the Scripture says:

9 – I was once alive apart from the law, but when the commandment came, sin came alive and I died.
10 – The very commandment that promised life proved to be death to me.
11 – For sin, seizing an opportunity through the commandment, deceived me and through it killed me.
12 – So the law is holy, and the commandment is holy and righteous and good.

Recognize what is noteworthy and true:

Paul's personification of the law here makes this doctrinal issue and problem sound like the plot of an intriguing murder mystery—a mystery Paul painstakingly solves for us. In verse 9, he revealed the starting point of this plot when saying, **"I was once alive apart from the law, but when the commandment came, sin came alive and I died."** This statement does not mean that we are spiritually alive apart from the law. Paul was saying that before God gave the law and before people placed their faith in Christ, they had no idea that we were spiritually dead and condemned by their sins. But now our awareness of the law can awaken and enable us to see that we are spiritually dead in our sins. It also stirs our sinful desire to rebel against the law, which only advances the death and destruction we can do to our lives. Thankfully, the law no longer strikes Christ-followers with this same death blow. Christ defeated death and sin for all who trust in Him, taking the sting out of death (1 Cor. 15:55-57).

In verse 10, Paul further explained the plot twist to this mystery, adding, **"The very commandment that promised life proved to be death to me."** Paul must have realized that no one would have seen this coming. The person who is oblivious to the law feels good—feels alive—before coming to know God's law. Unbelievers have no awareness of how truly depraved and sinful they are. Yet once people learn about the law, it proves deadly. We realize how dead we are in our sins without Christ. It's like when a man who feels fine, eats healthy, and regularly exercises discovers at a medical exam that he has stage 4 pancreatic cancer—the "Silent Killer." He assumed he would have much more time to live. In much the same way, without Christ, we have a silent killer within, but with Christ, we have the cure.

Paul echoed verse 8, saying in verse 11, **"For sin, seizing an opportunity through the commandment, deceived me and through it killed me."** Whenever we know God's laws and commandments, our sin natures are deceived and enticed to break those laws. Our sin nature tricks us into thinking sin is a good idea or beneficial choice. When we act on that temptation—taking the bait—we become like a fish caught on a line, reeled in to, at best, captivity and, at worst, death.

In verse 12, Paul reiterated the positive side of this truth regarding the law when he said, **"So the law is holy, and the commandment is holy and righteous and good."** Even though our sin nature becomes enticed to sin because of the law, our sins do not take away the holiness, righteousness, and goodness of the law. The law is our guide, pointing out when and how we are sinning. The law also helps awaken us to our spiritual condition. It helps us understand that we are dead in our sins, heightening our awareness of our need for Christ. From this vantage point, the law can bring an extremely "good" outcome even though it might cause pain in the process.

Thought to take:

The killer in this "murder mystery"—sin—remains at large and is on a murdering spree for all who are without Christ. Our only hope for identifying this deadly killer is to look to God's law and word. Thankfully, God takes our knowledge of His holy, good, and righteous law to open our eyes to our need for Him—for the salvation Christ offers. Some may still reject God and His law all of their lives, ultimately rejecting the hope of Christ. But I, for one, am happy to embrace God's law, word, and gospel. Now, the Spirit has replaced this silent killer's sting of death with the power to defeat every temptation life throws at me and us. So I will focus today on resisting sin by looking to and obeying God's law (reflecting on the 10 Commandments as one reference point). I will do all this in the Lord's power, knowing and rejoicing that He has already captured and arrested this silent killer. Through Christ, sin can no longer endanger my heart and life.

T2t: Resist sin and rely on God's law

Help from the Lord: Pray for God's help to apply your T2t both now and all day long.

Father, I am so grateful that You have taken care of every threat in my life, including the silent killer that Your law unmasks as my sin. I had no idea how dangerous my sin was when I was lost and ignorant of Your truth. And sometimes, even now, I forget how corrupting and destructive sin can be to my life, hindering the closeness of our relationship. So continually open my eyes to the destructiveness of sin and, conversely, the power and goodness of Your law. For, I am confident that Your law is what keeps me going in Your right and good direction, leading me toward more and more sanctification and Christlikeness! Always remind me to seek Your help when applying the law, since it is a task that only the Spirit can empower me to do and accomplish. Whenever I encounter temptation in this day, enable me to resist sin and choose You instead. Never let me give in to fear or hesitancy, knowing the sting of death cannot touch or penetrate my heart anymore because of what Your Son has won and done for me. Keep me from ever underestimating Your law, knowing how holy, good, and righteous it is and always will be. Use it today and every day to lead me to the feet of my holy, good, and righteous Savior! In Christ's precious name, amen.

Yield to the Lord: Throughout the day, yield your way for God's way, prayerfully reflecting on how you did at the end of your day.

20 – The Christian's Conundrum

Week 7, Day 2—Romans 7:13-15

Welcome the Lord!

Open my eyes, that I may behold wondrous things out of your law.
—Psalm 119:18

Observe what the Scripture says:

13 – Did that which is good, then, bring death to me? By no means! It was sin, producing death in me through what is good, in order that sin might be shown to be sin, and through the commandment might become sinful beyond measure.
14 – For we know that the law is spiritual, but I am of the flesh, sold under sin.
15 – For I do not understand my own actions. For I do not do what I want, but I do the very thing I hate.

Recognize what is noteworthy and true:

Paul continued to unpack the good side of the law and the horrible side of sin, saying: **"Did that which is good, then, bring death to me? By no means! It was sin, producing death in me through what is good, in order that sin might be shown to be sin, and through the commandment might become sinful beyond measure"** (v. 13). The Apostle knew that some might wrongly associate "that which is good" (meaning the law) with that which brings death. But that is the absolute wrong connection to make. Instead, it is our sin that produces death, even though the law reveals and arouses our sin nature to rebel against God (v. 5). Paul also revealed the depths to which our depravity can go, reminding us we "become sinful beyond measure" because the law arouses us to sin. However, we also must remember that the law shows (never causes) how we "might become sinful beyond measure." We are responsible for how we respond to the arousal of the law.

In verse 14, Paul contrasted the law and our sinful natures when he said, **"For we know that the law is spiritual, but I am of the flesh, sold under sin."** The law and humans are at odds whenever we operate in the flesh against a spiritual law. It is also important to note that there are two complementary meanings to the word "flesh" here. The first of these points to how incapable we are of keeping the law in the flesh, apart from Christ. The second points to our physical state—being human and of "flesh." Paul's present tense usage of "I am of the flesh" alludes to the former definition, identifying the struggle he faced daily to sin since his sin nature continued to tempt him to rebel against the law. He then punctuated this harsh reality, saying he was "sold under sin." This might seem to contradict Paul's position as a Christ-follower since, as a believer, he had become a slave "to Christ" and not "to sin." Perhaps he was focusing on the problem of believers trying to operate in the flesh, actively putting themselves under the authority of the law again. Or he might have been referring to the sin nature that remains active within both believers and unbelievers, since we all have been born in sin and must wrestle with it until the day we die. Regardless, both ring true and create ongoing battles in our lives.

In verse 15, Paul launched into a very relevant and vexing truth for every believer: **"For I do not understand my own actions. For I do not do what I want, but I do the very thing I hate."** Thankfully, the Spirit within believers arouses and stirs our desire to obey God—to keep His law. And like Paul said here, we often do not want to disobey God. But the Apostle could not understand why he—with a new heart and life in Christ—continued to do the very things he hated. Believers may no longer be enslaved to our sin nature, but we still feel the pull to sin, sinning even after being reborn in Christ. We are often tempted more intensely than unbelievers, especially as we come to know and study the law and God's word. But we must never forget that we now have the power through Christ to resist sin. If we do not realize and utilize what is available to us, it is a terrible waste of grace.

Thought to take:

We must never lose sight of two ways our sin nature deceives us. First, it can entice and deceive us into thinking we can keep the law in our human strength. Second, it can entice us to resist the law by giving in to our sinful nature and desires. But whenever we try to do these two things, we resist Christ and His authority. We act as if we are under the power and bondage of sin when Jesus has already set believers free. Jesus has already provided all the power and victory we need to defeat sin and temptation. We don't have to live with regret, choosing to sin and do the very things we, as Christ-followers, have come to hate through the

Spirit's illumination. With all of this in mind, my "Thought to take" for today will be to do what God wants—not what I want or think I can achieve on my own. If I'm ever in doubt as to what that is, I will look to God's law and word, asking the Father for the guidance and strength I need to choose His will over mine.

T2t: Do what God wants in His power

Help from the Lord: Pray for God's help to apply your T2t both now and all day long.

> Father, human beings, myself included, are so broken and beyond repair when we are without Your Spirit and truth to guide and empower us. I need only look to Your law to see where I fall short. Yet, when I do, I feel tempted to choose more brokenness and sin! Then I break Your law, which not only breaks down my heart and life but also breaks our fellowship. Help me recognize how foolish and insane these kinds of choices are. Help me view the problem of sin the way You do so that I am compelled to run to the safety of Your arms, receiving Your powerful grace to resist temptation. Remind me of the destruction that even one sin can bring to my life so I will choose a lifestyle of obedience rather than sinning beyond measure. In every crucial moment of this day, give me the answer to this confusing conundrum that is so unique to Christians. Give me the ability to obey–never giving in to the sin I hate but only coming to love You and Your law more and more with each step of obedience. And whenever I do resist You, whisper in my ear a tender and compelling call to return to You and Your way, giving me the power to run into Your arms. I want my heart to be completely Yours, the only Master who, paradoxically, gives me freedom in the bonds of grace. In Jesus' name, amen.

Yield to the Lord: Throughout the day, yield your way for God's way, prayerfully reflecting on how you did at the end of your day.

21 – The 'Intruder' Within

Week 7, Day 3—Romans 7:16-18

Welcome the Lord!

Observe what the Scripture says:

16 – Now if I do what I do not want, I agree with the law, that it is good.
17 – So now it is no longer I who do it, but sin that dwells within me.
18 – For I know that nothing good dwells in me, that is, in my flesh. For I have the desire to do what is right, but not the ability to carry it out.

Recognize what is noteworthy and true:

There are two main ways of understanding this section of Paul's teaching on the sin nature. It could be that Paul was speaking exclusively about every believer's spiritual battle (not just his own) since our sinful nature remains active even after we are born again. Or this could be about Paul's struggle with sin before coming to Christ. Either way, the law ignites the battle that rages within us, exposing the "outsider" leading this rebellion.

Paul spoke here to the Romans almost as if speaking to himself, sharing and processing out loud his inner thoughts each step of the way: **"Now if I do what I do not want, I agree with the law, that it is good"** (v. 16). He first restated how there are times when he chooses to do what he does not want to do by sinning (in both vv. 15 and 16). He then asserted how this actually shows his agreement with the law (v. 16). The desire to resist sin—to not want to do something evil—revealed the work of the law because it was convicting him in that regard. The law was allowing him to see that his sinful actions were wrong and corrupt. But the law went further for Paul—and still goes further for us—showing all the good that the law brings to our lives when we obey it.

In verse 17, Paul broke this sin process down even further so he could better examine and explain it, saying, **"So now it is no longer I who do it, but sin that dwells within me."** Even though Paul admitted he still struggled with sin as a believer (as do all believers), he also wanted to clarify that these sinful choices and attitudes do not come from his (or our) identity in Christ. He took this so far as to say he was no longer the one doing the sin but was compelled by his sin nature, describing this process as if an intruder was harassing him somehow inside his heart. He also emphasized how the sin nature dwells or resides within him and all believers, arousing us to give in to sin whenever temptation comes our way—which is all the time. We must remember that believers are no longer held under the authority of the sinful nature, unless we give it authority over us by sinning more and more. Our identity is in Christ and the indwelling sin nature no longer holds power over us as the redeemed. Standing in this truth helps us resist the harassing and deceptive voice of the "intruder" trying to squat within our hearts.

In verse 18, Paul again offered the deepest of humble confessions when he said, **"For I know that nothing good dwells in me, that is, in my flesh. For I have the desire to do what is right, but not the ability to carry it out."** We all must acknowledge and confess that absolutely "nothing good" dwells within our flesh since sin defiles all of our hearts. Our sin acts like raw sewage dumped into a freshwater supply, ruining it entirely. We cannot ignore the corruption our sins bring to our hearts and lives, knowing that doing so leads to more and more sinfulness. Try as we might, we cannot "do what is right"—resist sin—in our flesh (human strength). Facing this harsh reality leads us to our only Source—Christ—the One who gives us the strength to obey His will and law. No amount of human desire or power can accomplish this feat. It is far too big, daunting, and impossible for us without the help of our fully capable and all-powerful Lord.

Thought to take:

Although each person has a sinful nature within, because of what Christ has done, believers do not have to obey its harassing or deceptive voice. Our sin nature may be active within us but we do not need to view this oppositional nature as a guest, welcoming it in and allowing it to take over unguarded spaces in our hearts. As the redeemed, we must remember and stand on the truth that our identity is in Christ and our hearts belong to Him. Our lives should reflect the good that the law can do through us, giving all honor and glory for our obedience to our Savior. But this passage warns believers of a second factor always in play. We must resist listening to the intruder who tempts us to not only rely on our own flesh (human strength) to obey God but also tempts us to rebel against God's law altogether. That is why my aim for this day will be to turn away from the "intruder's" voice to turn toward the Spirit's voice. I will look to the law, God's word, and prayer to silence the "intruder's" call to sin, listening for what the Spirit wants to say instead.

T2t: Resist sin and "the outsider" (sin nature)

Help from the Lord: Pray for God's help to apply your T2t both now and all day long.

> Father, You know all about the intruder lurking, squatting, within my heart. But this intruder–my sin nature–is an authority that I no longer belong to, even though it still tries to call the shots in my life. You must be intimately and keenly aware of how often I hear sin calling out to me. For, I constantly feel it trying to win me back in both the subtlest and most enticing of ways, breaking down my will and desire to follow You. However, there are also times when I don't even know I'm opening the door to sin. I get distracted or grow hard-hearted in the worries and desires of life. In these weak moments, help me see the temptation for what it is so that I choose You instead. Also help me guard against sin in the future, coming to view my sin nature as the outsider and intruder it truly is. Still go further, reminding me that doing what I do not want to do–sinning–is a choice to go against Your sweet Spirit and good law. You are the only One who can help me resist the siren call of sin. The only One strong enough to silence the harassing and intimidating voice that shouts within my heart and mind each day. Enable me to remember that my sin nature was a tyrant in my life at one time, but no longer is my master nor can control me. Thank You for disarming this intruder when You redeemed me and took hold of my heart through Your salvation and grace. Now, I only want to celebrate and embrace Your law because I see how it illuminates my path and gives me the boundary lines for leading an abundant, Christ-honoring life. I promise to lean into You and Your law today and every day. Use my faithfulness to reflect Your goodness and grace to those who need Your truth, guidance, and salvation like I so desperately do. In Christ's name, amen.

Yield to the Lord: Throughout the day, yield your way for God's way, prayerfully reflecting on how you did at the end of your day.

Week Seven Questions for Discussion or Contemplation

Read aloud week seven's passage, Romans 7:9-13 ...

1. What are some ways your sin nature has deceived you in the past (v. 11)?

2. Refer to the Ten Commandments (Ex. 20:3-17) for your answer to this question: What particular law has brought much good to your life and in what way (vv. 12-13)?

3. What do you think the law arouses us to be "sinful beyond measure" means (v. 13)? What or who is ultimately responsible for this outcome?

4. What are the truths or truth principles we might not have talked about yet from verses 9-13 that catch your attention, and why?

Read aloud week seven's passage, Romans 7:14-18 ...

5. Since we all are "of the flesh," how can we know when we are following the law in God's strength or trying to follow it in our own (v. 14)? Brainstorm all the ways we can gain awareness of our tendency to operate in our own strength.

6. What are some tendencies to sin that you "hate" in your life (v. 15), and why?

7. How does knowing God's word and the law work to fire up this inner battle within you (v. 15-18)? Does this give you less or more of a desire to know the law since it brings conviction of sin? Explain.

8. How would you explain the positive side of this truth—"nothing good dwells in me"—to someone who feels God's word is harsh and condemning (v. 18)? What is ultimately being said here?

9. What are the truths or truth principles we might not have talked about yet from verses 14-18 that catch your attention, and why?

10. What is one thing from this past week's study that you want to learn from and live out more?

11. Would anyone like to read a prayer you wrote based on one of the Scriptures from this week? How can we pray for you?

Week Eight

22 – Dreadful Versus Delightful

Week 8, Day 1—Romans 7:19-22

Welcome the Lord!

Open my eyes, that I may behold wondrous things out of your law.
—Psalm 119:18

Observe what the Scripture says:

19 – For I do not do the good I want, but the evil I do not want is what I keep on doing.
20 – Now if I do what I do not want, it is no longer I who do it, but sin that dwells within me.
21 – So I find it to be a law that when I want to do right, evil lies close at hand.
22 – For I delight in the law of God, in my inner being,

Recognize what is noteworthy and true:

Paul continued to wrestle with all sides of this sin problem with these thoughts in verse 19, **"For I do not do the good I want, but the evil I do not want is what I keep on doing."** This statement is almost identical to what he said in verse 15, likely reiterated here to emphasize this monumental inner and daily struggle against the sin nature. Paul acknowledged that the indwelling Spirit stirred him to want to do good. In contrast, he also felt the pull to do evil, finding himself doing evil even though Christ had given him a new heart through salvation. This struggle is active and constant for every believer. Our hearts and motivations truly have changed through Christ's regenerative work. Still, our sin nature continually tries to steer us back toward our former lives when we were unbelievers, dominated and controlled by sin.

In verse 20, Paul reiterated his thought from earlier (v. 17), saying, **"Now if I do what I do not want, it is no longer I who do it, but sin that dwells within me."** Paul characterized the sin nature like an intruder in verse 17. But, today, allow me to take it in a different direction, viewing the sin nature like I've characterized it before as a cancer lurking within our bodies. For example, a man who has cancer will still want to do "good things"—stay active, eat well, and keep up his regular routines, even though all of this will be harder to do with cancer in his body. In a similar way, our sin nature makes it harder for us to do what is good and right. And we dare not think that Paul was shirking his responsibility when he said, "it is no longer I who do it." Instead, he was highlighting how his choice to sin does not stem from his identity in Christ. Like "cancer" does not define the one afflicted, our sin nature dwells within but does not define believers nor remove our identity in Christ. Best of all, Christ provides salvation, ultimately curing this cancerous disease of sin. He helps us resist sin now and, in eternity one day, will perfect and glorify us through Him, allowing us to stand sinless before His throne (Rom. 8:29-30; 2 Cor. 3:18; Phil. 3:20-21; Col. 3:4).

In verse 21, Paul drew an interesting conclusion about this struggle: **"So I find it to be a law that when I want to do right, evil lies close at hand."** Paul's challenge of wanting to do right, even as evil is right there beside him, felt just as active and compelling to him as the law of God did when it aroused him to sin This particular law is the same one Paul mentioned in Romans 6:13, 7:5, and 7:23—the law that is active within our "members" (v. 5). Since the law is within our members, it always feels "close at hand." The members or parts of our body—eyes, ears, lips, hands, feet, mind, etc.—are what we are tempted to use to sin.

Like a pendulum, Paul swung back to the opposite side of this sin problem with these positive words, **"For I delight in the law of God, in my inner being,"** (v. 22). As a Christ-follower, Paul not only wanted to do good but he also delighted in doing God's law. He also stressed where this delight comes from and originates for himself and all believers—in the inner being. In other words, the source of Paul's delight came from the indwelling of the Spirit who anchors the believer's identity in Christ. As a believer, when you delight in the law and desire to follow it—bringing God the glory—the Lord empowers you to both delight in and do those things from the inner being—your identity in Christ. The impossible is accomplished through the power of the Spirit who dwells in your heart.

T hought to take:

Believers and unbelievers alike feel the dreadful pull toward sin every day of our lives. Thankfully, as believers, this does not mean we are defeated by it nor too weak—through the Spirit—to resist temptation when it comes to call. In those crucial moments, you and I must remember all Christ has done and won for us to arrest and—one day, in eternity—completely cure us of this cancerous sin nature.

So, like Paul, I want to rely on the Spirit, knowing He resides in my inner being. I will also delight in God's law by joyfully surrendering my way for Christ's and thanking Him for giving me the power through His word to resist temptation. In every way that I resist sin, I will confirm my delight for God's law by glorifying Christ rather than drawing praise or approval for myself.

T2t: Delight in God's law

Help from the Lord: Pray for God's help to apply your T2t both now and all day long.

> *Father, I thank You for providing Your inner guidance and strength for dealing with the cancerous effects of the sin nature. You are not leaving me alone to figure this problem out for myself. You are by my side. No, even better! You are within me, holding me steady and enabling me to resist sin every time I feel weak and tempted. In a strange way, this makes my struggle against sin sweeter rather than bitter. That's because I know You are closer at hand than even my sinful nature lurking within my mind and members. You are stronger than the convicting force of the law. And You are more powerful than my sin nature even as it continually pulls me toward evil and the patterns of my past unredeemed life. Now, I have every reason to rejoice in how You have transformed my mind and motivations through Your Son. Because of this, I not only want to follow Your law but You increase my delight in Your law with each obedient choice I make. So, as I commit myself today to relying more completely on Your Spirit, deepen my desire to choose Your desires over my own while also deepening and manifesting my delight in Your law. Make it so reflective of who I am that others don't see me nearly as much as they see You shining through in my eyes, words, actions, attitude, and life. In Jesus' name, amen.*

Yield to the Lord: Throughout the day, yield your way for God's way, prayerfully reflecting on how you did at the end of your day.

23 – Death Defying

Week 8, Day 2—Romans 7:23-25

Welcome the Lord!

Open my eyes, that I may behold wondrous things out of your law.
—Psalm 119:18

Observe what the Scripture says:

23 – but I see in my members another law waging war against the law of my mind and making me captive to the law of sin that dwells in my members.
24 – Wretched man that I am! Who will deliver me from this body of death?
25 – Thanks be to God through Jesus Christ our Lord! So then, I myself serve the law of God with my mind, but with my flesh I serve the law of sin.

Recognize what is noteworthy and true:

Paul mentioned the law of God earlier, in verse 22, continuing here in verse 23 to contrast it with the law of sin: **"but I see in my members another law waging war against the law of my mind and making me captive to the law of sin that dwells in my members."** Verse 23 also dovetails nicely with the teaching found in Ephesians 6:10-18 on spiritual warfare. However, at this juncture, Paul emphasized the battle that wages within us rather than discussing how evil forces attack us from the outer spiritual realm. The Apostle likely focused on "the law of the mind" here because we use our minds to decide whether to disobey or obey God. Like the evil forces in the spiritual or heavenly realm, the law of sin acts like an enemy, constantly waging war against our minds and the desire to follow Christ. Even more chilling, this "enemy" (law of sin) can capture our minds—making us prisoners of an unrelenting inner war. Still, this captivity can only come when we try to battle temptation in our own strength rather than in the overcoming power of Christ's Spirit. Thankfully, our Savior has set us free from the domination of sin and our sin nature.

In verse 24, Paul gave voice to his struggle against the law of sin with this poignant and pain-filled declaration: **"Wretched man that I am! Who will deliver me from this body of death?"** The Greek word that Paul used here for "wretched" refers to being exhausted from working so hard, referring to the many times he had tried to obey the law in his own strength. He might also be alluding to how tired he was of fighting the law of sin, which pulled him toward sin even after being redeemed by Christ. This realization and plea—"who will deliver me"—shows how desperate Paul was for his Savior's help. And the additional phrase—"from this body of death"—paints an awful portrait of how massively devastating sin can be to our lives. It might be possible that Paul was thinking here of an ancient custom that tyrants sometimes used, punishing prisoners by tying them to a dead body. This idea captures the harsh reality of how we can spiritually chain ourselves to a corpse of sorts when we choose to sin.

In verse 25, Paul turned from the dark side of this battle to the victorious and joyful side: **"Thanks be to God through Jesus Christ our Lord! So then, I myself serve the law of God with my mind, but with my flesh I serve the law of sin."** The Greek word Paul used for "thanks" here is "charis" (meaning grace). Out of thanks, Paul wanted God to receive the same grace that the Lord had given him when He delivered Paul from captivity to sin. Paul also emphasized that this grace (helping power) is only accessible through Jesus. He went on to summarize how this spiritual tug-of-war operates. One end of the rope represents when Paul served (surrendered) his mind to the law, becoming "captive to" (captivated by) the law of God. The other end of the rope represents when Paul's flesh (sin nature) pulled him in the opposite direction to serve the law of sin. Continually allowing God to renew and conform our minds to His law and truth can help us win this tug-of-war. When we turn the reins over to Him, we receive the grace (strength) to resist the law of sin and are pulled back to His side (Rom. 12:2; 2 Cor. 10:4-5).

Thought to take:

I really appreciate the transparency and courage Paul displayed here, confessing his inner battle with the law of sin. If any human could have resisted this pull—other than Christ—it had to have been the rock-steady, sold-out, imprisoned and persecuted Apostle Paul. Yet this passage brings to light how much he must have struggled inwardly each day to resist sin, choosing to follow and obey God instead. This is a daily challenge for every believer since we all feel the tension between both the sinful nature—living as an intruder within us—and the indwelling Spirit of God convicting and drawing us toward His law. Ultimately, we can let sin take us captive. Or we can allow God and His word to captivate our hearts, where, paradoxically, we experience the greatest freedom possible.

I want to give myself wholeheartedly to the pursuit of God's law today, relying on the grace of Christ that gives me the power to resist sin. So whenever I feel this tension and struggle emerging in my life, I will surrender my mind and thoughts to God for Him to conform to His truth and law. At those times, I will thank God for helping me with His grace and power to resist the temptation to sin.

T2t: Let God captivate my mind

Help from the Lord: Pray for God's help to apply your T2t both now and all day long.

Father, I can relate so much to Paul's struggle with sin. I know that insidious inner enemy of the sinful nature all too well. I feel this unwanted desire to surrender to the sin nature every day. I'm very familiar with how it wages war in my mind, pulling me away from the good and right desire to follow Your law. Most of the time, I know Your law and what You want me to do. I even know how to escape. But when I don't, it's just a matter of searching out Your truth in the pages of Your word and applying it to my life when the heat is on. But far too often I take the lazy route. And when I do, it is as if I take the hand of this body of death—a putrid and decaying corpse of sin—to walk away from You and Your law. What a wretched choice! But it's a choice I never have to make again. So give me the power and motivation to surrender my mind to You, receiving the power of Christ to resist sins of every kind. There are really only two choices in this life—to choose death and sin or to choose You and Your law. One way holds me captive in a dungeon, handcuffed to the rotting corpse of my sin nature. The other captivates my heart and truly sets me free to live out Your best, sovereign plan for my life. Apply Your good and pure law to my heart, Lord, dousing the flames of sinful desire that rage within. Captivate my heart and conform my mind to what springs from and mirrors Your mind. Thank You for a bond that is never restrictive—only comforting, secure, and wrapped in the power and goodness of Your grace. In Christ's name, amen.

Yield to the Lord: Throughout the day, yield your way for God's way, prayerfully reflecting on how you did at the end of your day.

24 – Right and Might

Week 8, Day 3—Romans 8:1-4

Welcome the Lord!

Open my eyes, that I may behold wondrous things out of your law.
—Psalm 119:18

Observe what the Scripture says:

1 – There is therefore now no condemnation for those who are in Christ Jesus.
2 – For the law of the Spirit of life has set you free in Christ Jesus from the law of sin and death.
3 – For God has done what the law, weakened by the flesh, could not do. By sending his own Son in the likeness of sinful flesh and for sin, he condemned sin in the flesh,
4 – in order that the righteous requirement of the law might be fulfilled in us, who walk not according to the flesh but according to the Spirit.

Recognize what is noteworthy and true:

This passage marks a climax in the gospel message that Paul has shared thus far. It is a high point—a mountaintop—with Paul summarizing the Christ-follower's faith with this iconic and reassuring verse: **"There is therefore now no condemnation for those who are in Christ Jesus"** (v. 1). What an incredible truth and reality! "Those who are in Christ Jesus"—the redeemed—are now no longer condemned by God. Our Savior took on the condemnation that should have been ours when He died on the cross. He did the redeeming work, allowing believers to simply rest through faith in what He has accomplished for us. And because of Christ's redemption, believers never have to listen to condemning words or thoughts either. God convicts us of sin, but the evil one uses condemnation instead to disorient and crush the believer even though condemnation no longer applies because we are "in Christ."

In verse 2, Paul further explained what being "in Christ" includes, saying, **"For the law of the Spirit of life has set you free in Christ Jesus from the law of sin and death."** The law of the Spirit is more than enough—is sufficient—for setting "those who are in Christ" free from the law of sin and death. In what way does Christ do this? First, verse 1 tells us that Christ has set believers free from the guilt and punishment of sin—we are no longer condemned. Second, verse 2 tells us that "in Christ" and through the Spirit, believers have been set free from the binding power and authority of the law of sin and death.

Paul then further explained what God did to save the lost: **"For God has done what the law, weakened by the flesh, could not do. By sending his own Son in the likeness of sinful flesh and for sin, he condemned sin in the flesh,"** (v. 3). God knew that we, in our weak flesh, could never fulfill or completely follow the law. Because of this weakness, God sent His own Son in the likeness of (appearing like) man to accomplish for us what we could not. Paul also emphasized in verse 3 that Jesus came "in the likeness of flesh" to explain how Christ took on the form of a fully human man yet was without sin and fully divine. The Father could condemn sin through His Son's death because Jesus came in the form of a man, identified with us, and went through all that we experience without sinning. He was the perfect sacrifice, enabling the Father to condemn sin in the flesh of His Son while Christ hung on the cross, taking the punishment we deserved. Because of this, Jesus accomplished something the law was unequipped or incapable of doing—saving the lost.

In verse 4, Paul then described what Christ's work on the cross did for us, adding, **"in order that the righteous requirement of the law might be fulfilled in us, who walk not according to the flesh but according to the Spirit."** Christ met the righteous requirement of the law through His sinless life, providing the substitutionary atonement and righteousness for "those who are in Christ." Because of this, God can look at the redeemed and not condemn us for our sins (v. 1). When the Father looks at us, He only sees Christ and His righteousness. Now, we can walk not according to the flesh but living our lives according to and in cooperation with the Spirit. The emphasis in verse 4 is on how Christ empowers the faith walk (sanctification) of believers, which contrasts with and adds to what Paul declared in verse 1 regarding the believer's position in Christ (salvation).

Thought to take:

Theologian William Manson said of this Bible passage, "Moses' law has right but not might; sin's law has might but not right; the law of the Spirit has both right and might." Manson accurately summarized what Paul revealed and confirmed for us here. The Mosaic law and our flesh are too weak to save us. But through Christ's work on the cross, believers are joined *in Him*—made right through Jesus' might and righteousness. Our part is to rest and rely each day in His might and righteousness. This means we must embrace the truth that Jesus has set believers free from the domination of sin. It also means relying on the Spirit's might and strength to live according to and in cooperation with God's law and Holy Spirit. Today, I will rejoice that Christ has set me free from sin—making me "right" in God's eyes. I will also live according to the Spirit, resisting temptation with the LORD's overcoming might.

T2t: Resist sin and follow God

Help from the Lord: Pray for God's help to apply your T2t both now and all day long.

> Father, I stand in awe of You, moved with heartfelt gratitude for how You saved me through Your Son's mightiness and righteousness. Being seen by You without condemnation, even though I have sinned against You time and time again, both humbles and relieves me. No doubt Your redemptive plan came at such a high and painful cost to You and Your Son, yet You gave freely and without reserve. Use my growing understanding of how costly and unmerited this gift is—my salvation and righteousness through Christ—as a way to keep me from ever underestimating or questioning Your love. Enable me to always rise up in Your strength, resisting sin by living out Your law and walking out my salvation. Keep me aware of times when I lose sight of this freedom and might, moving me to grab hold of Your ever-present power to resist sin once again. Remind me, in those dark hours, that there is no challenge, barrier, or restriction in my life that can take Your freedom and might away from me! Stir up Your Spirit within, inspiring me to rejoice in the freedom Christ has given me. Then use my joy to fire up even greater devotion to You so that I follow You alone and never return to the captivity of sin and shame. Empower me to reflect Christ and His glory today, knowing Your redemption of my heart looks so incredibly glorious to all who see me living out Your law and truth. In Christ's name, amen.

Yield to the Lord: Throughout the day, yield your way for God's way, prayerfully reflecting on how you did at the end of your day.

Week Eight Questions for Discussion or Contemplation

Read aloud Day 1, Romans 7:19-22 ...

1. What is a situation in your life that typically puts you in the same frame of mind as Paul talked about in verse 19—not doing the good you want to do, while doing the evil you don't want to do? How do you relate to Paul's frustration and bewilderment?

2. Let's brainstorm! What are some ways we can "delight" in or come to delight in God's law (v. 22)?

3. What are the truths or truth principles we might not have talked about yet from verses 19-22 that catch your attention, and why?

Read aloud Day 2, Romans 7:23-25 ...

4. How does it feel to know there are two battles waging against you in the spiritual realm—an outer battle with evil spirits and an inner battle waging because of your sinful nature (v. 23)?

5. What types of "grace" (God's help and empowerment) do you need to serve the law of God with your mind in a difficult situation in your life (v. 25)? Answer this way: I need His "help" to ...

6. What are the truths or truth principles we might not have talked about yet from verses 23-25 that catch your attention, and why?

Read aloud Day 3, Romans 8:1-4 ...

7. What have been some condemning thoughts others have said to you or that you've entertained? How does verse 1 change your perspective about those thoughts and whether they are true for you?

8. Why did Jesus need to come "in the likeness of sinful flesh" (vv. 3-4)? What do you appreciate most about the fact that Christ physically came in human form for the redeemed?

9. What are the truths or truth principles we might not have talked about yet from verses 1-4 that catch your attention, and why?

10. What is one thing from this past week's study that you want to learn from and live out more?

11. Would anyone like to read a prayer you wrote based on one of the Scriptures from this week? How can we pray for you?

Week Nine

25 – Set on Life or Death?

Week 9, Day 1—Romans 8:5-7

Welcome the Lord!

Open my eyes, that I may behold wondrous things out of your law.
—Psalm 119:18

Observe what the Scripture says:

5 – For those who live according to the flesh set their minds on the things of the flesh, but those who live according to the Spirit set their minds on the things of the Spirit.
6 – For to set the mind on the flesh is death, but to set the mind on the Spirit is life and peace.
7 – For the mind that is set on the flesh is hostile to God, for it does not submit to God's law; indeed, it cannot.

Recognize what is noteworthy and true:

Paul continued to teach here on the subject of "the flesh" (v. 4), identifying a clear connection that must be made: **"For those who live according to the flesh set their minds on the things of the flesh,"** (v. 5a). "Those who live according to the flesh" describes an unbeliever's lifestyle dominated by and taken captive to the law of sin (v. 2). This problematic mindset describes what Peter was tempted to embrace when Jesus strongly rebuked him for not setting his mind on the things of God (Mt. 16:23). Even one of Jesus' closest and most fervent disciples proved how easy it is to be deceived, thinking this mindset is correct or good. Thankfully, the Spirit within believers keeps us from continuing to "live according the flesh," always helping to reset our minds on Christ.

Paul followed up this line of reasoning, adding, **"but those who live according to the Spirit set their minds on the things of the Spirit"** (v. 5b). "Those who live according to the Spirit" describes believers who live lives and lifestyles led and controlled by the Spirit. Believers still struggle with sin every day but never stray from God too far, nor for very long. The Spirit works constantly to draw the wayward believer back to repentance. Those who do not eventually return should prayerfully consider whether they are truly trusting in Christ for salvation.

In verse 6, Paul identified the outcome of these two opposing walks and lifestyles, saying, **"For to set the mind on the flesh is death, but to set the mind on the Spirit is life and peace."** Paul did not say here that setting our minds on the flesh leads to death but rather "is death"—ultimately, equating it with death. People who set their minds on the flesh have become possessed and controlled by sin—demonstrating that they are spiritually dead unbelievers who will face "death" for all eternity. When we reject God's ways, both unbelievers and believers experience "death" in other ways—death to our good works, to satisfying relationships, to satisfaction in life, etc. In contrast, when we, as believers, set our minds on the Spirit, life and peace come to our hearts, actions, and relationships, including our relationship with God.

In verse 7, Paul explained why the flesh opposes the Spirit when he said, **"For the mind that is set on the flesh is hostile to God, for it does not submit to God's law; indeed, it cannot."** The Greek word Paul used for hostile here means "enmity." Those who set their minds on the flesh rather than submitting to God's law and word are enemies of and hostile toward God. Since believers are not enemies of God, some believe this means Paul was talking specifically here about unbelievers. Regardless, true believers can sometimes act like enemies of God by resisting His law, though this never severs our relationship with Him. This verse also illustrates how the flesh (sin nature) produces death, blocking a person's ability to submit to God's law. If you or I try to do this, it's like relying on a corpse to get up and do the work God is calling us to do. It is a foolish idea and a futile plan.

Thought to take:

This passage holds both a powerful warning and a command. The warning reminds us that we cannot follow God's law or live for Him without setting our minds on the things of the Spirit and living according to (relying fully on) the Spirit. The lives of those who live according to the flesh—pursuing a "lifestyle" focused on themselves rather than God—point to being unregenerate unbelievers. Those who consistently set their minds on the things of the Spirit demonstrate that they are Christ-followers. Pursuing the flesh leads to death but pursuing the Spirit leads to life and peace in our actions, attitudes, and relationships. I know which Person and direction I want to pursue and reflect! I will strive to set my mind on the things of the Spirit, relying on Christ and waiting on Him to produce the life and peace I desperately need.

T2t: Set mind on the Spirit

Help **from the Lord:** Pray for God's help to apply your T2t both now and all day long.

> *Father, this passage makes it abundantly clear that I cannot rely on my human understanding or fleshly strength to follow or accomplish Your law. Not only is this a foolish idea and futile plan but it is also the worst insult to You and Your grace! When I set my mind on the flesh, giving in to my human desires, I act like Your enemy. So whenever my flesh cries out for something different than what You have provided—wake me up to the awfulness of this desire. Make it clear to me that, when I choose my way over Yours, I am rejecting You, essentially, spitting in Your face. When I fall prey to this thinking, use Your Spirit to woo me back to Your side, taking these sinful and human desires captive so that my mind stays fully set on You alone. Unleash Your Spirit to control my every thought, attitude, and action. Then bring life to all I do for You—all I experience because of You. Allow Your peace to flow through my heart in these moments of surrender, convincing me and all who see my life that You are the Source of all that is good, fruitful, and righteous in life. In Jesus' name, amen.*

Yield **to the Lord:** Throughout the day, yield your way for God's way, prayerfully reflecting on how you did at the end of your day.

26 - Signs of Life

Week 9, Day 2—Romans 8:8-10

Welcome the Lord!

Open my eyes, that I may behold wondrous things out of your law.
—Psalm 119:18

Observe what the Scripture says:

8 – Those who are in the flesh cannot please God.
9 – You, however, are not in the flesh but in the Spirit, if in fact the Spirit of God dwells in you. Anyone who does not have the Spirit of Christ does not belong to him.
10 – But if Christ is in you, although the body is dead because of sin, the Spirit is life because of righteousness.

Recognize what is noteworthy and true:

Paul left us with little doubt about the outcome of this common spiritual problem when he boldly declared in verse 8, **"Those who are in the flesh cannot please God."** Paul was referring to unbelievers exclusively when he referenced, "Those who are in the flesh."* Although believers occasionally try to please God out of human strength (flesh), this is not what Paul was talking about here. The Apostle took this issue deeper saying this is the person who is "in the flesh." This phrase describes someone who has set their mind and lifestyle on the flesh (human will and strength), which makes this person "hostile to God" (v. 7).

In verse 9, Paul drew a line between unbelievers and believers when he said: **"You, however, are not in the flesh but in the Spirit, if in fact the Spirit of God dwells in you. Anyone who does not have the Spirit of Christ does**

not belong to him." Paul first clarified that those who operate "not in the flesh but in the Spirit" are believers. He then added a curious caveat, "if in fact the Spirit of God dwells in you." He made this distinction to remind us that it is only through the indwelling Spirit of God—being "in the Spirit"—that we are able to consistently live out and display God's power. This reality and statement also assure believers of our salvation because the Spirit of God dwells "in us" and is not just working externally. Ever wonder how believers can know that we belong to Christ and have the Spirit within us? Part of the answer is found in the context of chapter 8 (particularly in verse 5) when Paul said, "those who live according to the Spirit set their minds on the things of the Spirit." God empowers believers controlled by the Spirit to resist basing their lives and choices on the desires of the flesh. God empowers us to desire what He desires and enables us to accomplish His will through His strength. When we consistently feel the desire to resist and do resist the nagging cry of the flesh, we give evidence of the Spirit's control and transformation of our hearts.

In verse 10, Paul reveals what the Spirit does within the believer, **"But if Christ is in you, although the body is dead because of sin, the Spirit is life because of righteousness."** The Greek word for "if" in this verse can also be translated as "since," revealing Paul's confidence in the salvation of many in this church. Interestingly, Paul used the Greek word "soma" for "body" in this verse to highlight all that makes us human, including our physical parts or "members" (v. 7:23). As long as we live in these bodies, we will never escape the pull to use different parts of our bodies to sin. Thankfully, the indwelling Spirit gives believers spiritual "life" through Christ's "righteousness," enabling us to resist sin and sinful lifestyles. Christ's righteousness is actually "imputed" to believers, capturing the idea of God putting the riches of Christ's holiness into our "spiritual bank accounts" (Rom. 4:5; 2 Cor. 5:21). This makes us rich beyond measure.

Thought to take:

This Scripture passage confirms two important truths. First, we cannot please God by being "in the flesh." Second, if we have the Spirit of God within us, we can resist sin and the pull of the flesh because of Christ's righteousness and power filling our hearts and lives. We gain assurance that we belong to Christ when our desires mirror His and our lives give evidence of consistent cooperation with His Spirit. The Spirit also convinces us that we never need to add something to what Christ has already done perfectly for us through His righteousness. I'm just so grateful that Jesus covers me with His righteousness, offering me the most abundant life ever as I rest in His strength. So whenever I'm tempted today to yield to my human, flesh-based desires, I will remember whose I am—Christ's! I will rely on Him to strengthen me to walk away from sin, thanking Him for giving me this power through His life and righteousness.

T2t: I am Christ's—rely on Him

Help from the Lord: Pray for God's help to apply your T2t both now and all day long.

> *Father, it is such a joy to know that I belong to You! To know that You have covered me with Christ's righteousness and are stirring up life in me and the things I do in Your strength. Keep this truth and reality front and center in my mind, empowering me to set my mind on the Spirit at all times. Never let me fall for the lie that I can do something good or helpful without You, or that I have enough strength and wisdom to gain some desire apart from You. Empty my heart of every self-centered thought that tempts me to operate independently of You—in hostility to You. And when the seductive song of temptation whispers in my ear, help me remember that relying on human desires only brings deception and destruction. Remind me that these things promise so much delight but, in the end, become like a kiss from a corpse, rotting and long-dead. In contrast, walking in Your Spirit brings life to everything I do for You, leaving me convinced that Your way is best! So, as I walk in the Spirit today, use each act of obedience as a way to confirm to me and others that You are at work in my life and present in my heart. And I will give You all the praise and thanks both now and in the future for doing what my corrupt and dead flesh could never do—bring glory to Your Son! In Christ's name, amen.*

Yield to the Lord: Throughout the day, yield your way for God's way, prayerfully reflecting on how you did at the end of your day.

*Refer to this link for further clarification - https://www.biblword.net/can-non-christians-do-good-works/

27 – Empty Hands

Week 9, Day 3—Romans 8:11-13

Welcome the Lord!

Open my eyes, that I may behold wondrous things out of your law.
—Psalm 119:18

Observe what the Scripture says:

11 – If the Spirit of him who raised Jesus from the dead dwells in you, he who raised Christ Jesus from the dead will also give life to your mortal bodies through his Spirit who dwells in you.
12 – So then, brothers, we are debtors, not to the flesh, to live according to the flesh.
13 – For if you live according to the flesh you will die, but if by the Spirit you put to death the deeds of the body, you will live.

Recognize what is noteworthy and true:

Paul communicated his confidence in the faith of these Roman believers once again, saying, **"If [Since] the Spirit of him who raised Jesus from the dead dwells in you, he who raised Christ Jesus from the dead will also give life to your mortal bodies through his Spirit who dwells in you"** (v. 11). The statement "the Spirit of him" refers not only to the Spirit's work in Christ's resurrection but also to the Father's part in this miraculous feat. However, other Scriptures remind us that all three, acting as one God, were involved in raising Christ from the dead (Jn. 10:17-18; 2 Cor. 4:14; Gal. 1:1). Each Person of the trinity—including Christ—played a particular, yet inseparable, role in our redemption. Paul then reiterated the truth that the Spirit of God gives our mortal bodies "life" as the Spirit comes to dwell within those who trust in Christ for salvation. We are spiritually dead until the "Spirit of him" resurrects our human spirits when we are saved. Believers' "mortal bodies" will also be resurrected when Christ returns for His own (8:23-24).

In verse 12, Paul put the gift of God—our salvation and the indwelling Spirit—into perspective when he said, **"So then, brothers, we are debtors, not to the flesh, to live according to the flesh."** The Apostle wanted to clarify what we owe because of the new life we have gained through Christ's salvation. Although we are "debtors," we owe nothing to our human flesh and everything to Christ. We owe our lives to our Savior because He sacrificed His perfect, righteous life for ours. Therefore, we have an obligation to resist the flesh, avoiding living according to its sinful pull by relying instead on the Spirit to obey God.

In verse 13, Paul reiterated the difference between being unregenerate and regenerate through the Spirit when he said, **"For if you live according to the flesh you will die, but if by the Spirit you put to death the deeds of the body, you will live."** When unbelievers choose to live according to the flesh—trusting in their human desires rather than in Christ—they are ultimately pursuing death. Choosing this way not only keeps them spiritually dead and separated from the Spirit but also means they will experience eternal death—finding themselves separated from God in hell forever. Believers can choose to act according to the flesh too but cannot *live* according to the flesh—remaining in that deeply sinful state for long. Lastly, Paul emphasized how living by the Spirit means putting to death the deeds of the body by dying to our human desires, particularly when these contradict or supersede our desire for God and His desires. We never lose anything that matters by choosing God's way since He brings life to all we are and all we do when we live by the Spirit. This is living not only in the truth but *truly* living.

Thought to take:

Paul's words here remind us that we should never take for granted "the life" we, as believers, experience in Christ. We should never yield to any selfish desires since these tempt us to reject Christ and His resurrection power, bringing death to all God wants to do in and through us as the redeemed. As debtors to Christ, we must stop and truly consider what we are doing when we choose our own way over God's way. The painful surrender of our desires means gaining Christ's abundant life—both now and in eternity. Yet this is a life that only empty hands can hold and embrace. So today, I will remember that I owe Christ my life, allowing this realization to move me to surrender my desires—"put to death the deeds of the body"—so the Spirit can bring life to all I do for my Savior.

T2t: Die to myself and live for God

Help from the Lord: Pray for God's help to apply your T2t both now and all day long.

> *Father, I want to rejoice in the resurrection, rejoicing in both the resurrection of Christ's body and the many ways You have resurrected my mortal body. You have brought to life my heart and mind, enabling me to know and long for You and what You desire above any desire I might have in the flesh. That alone is a miracle in and of itself! Soften my heart to know just how hostile and insulting it is to You when I choose myself over You. Use this to draw me back to You and Your desires. I also need You to stir up my love and appreciation for Christ's salvation so I recognize just how undeserving I am to receive such a grace-empowered and life-transformational gift. Use my gratitude for Christ to deepen my devotion, compelling me to give all I can and all I am each and every day for Your Son's sake and glory. Enable me to constantly turn to Your indwelling Spirit for the power to follow You. As I do, I will sing Your praises all day long, trusting in and counting every way You bring to life more of Yourself through my life. Keep my hands empty, surrendering my way for Yours, allowing me to receive all You want to resurrect and invigorate in and through my life and those my life touches. In Jesus' name, amen.*

Yield to the Lord: Throughout the day, yield your way for God's way, prayerfully reflecting on how you did at the end of your day.

Week Nine Questions for Discussion or Contemplation

Read aloud Day 1, Romans 8:5-7 …

1. What are some signs that a person is setting his or her mind on the Spirit (v. 5)? How would you rate your own life (0 being not at all to 5 being very evident) based on these signs?

2. What do you think it means that an unbeliever "cannot" submit to God's law (v. 7)? How do you think God feels about the good someone might do whose mind is "set on the flesh"? Why?

3. What are the truths or truth principles we might not have talked about yet from verses 5-7 that catch your attention, and why?

Read aloud Day 2, Romans 8:8-10 …

4. Why would people who are "in the flesh" (unbelievers) want to do good OR want to please God (v. 8)? Why is choosing to "live in the flesh so insulting to God?

5. Have you ever struggled with feeling assured of your salvation and what made you doubt it? How can verse 10 give someone greater confidence that Christ is in them—that they are saved?

6. What are the truths or truth principles we might not have talked about yet from verses 8-10 that catch your attention, and why?

Read aloud Day 3, Romans 8:11-13 …

7. What are some of the wonderful implications of verse 11 that people might overlook? What can you do to further integrate the reality that you possess Christ's resurrection power?

8. Give specific examples of "deeds of the body" from people in general, and if you're brave enough, from your life. How can you and I improve on putting these to death (v. 13)?

9. What are the truths or truth principles we might not have talked about yet from verses 11-13 that catch your attention, and why?

10. What is one thing from this past week's study that you want to learn from and live out more?

11. Would anyone like to read a prayer you wrote based on one of the Scriptures from this week? How can we pray for you?

Week Ten

28 – Who's Your Daddy?

Week 10, Day 1—Romans 8:14-16

Welcome the Lord!

Open my eyes, that I may behold wondrous things out of your law.
—Psalm 119:18

Observe what the Scripture says:

14 – For all who are led by the Spirit of God are sons of God.
15 – For you did not receive the spirit of slavery to fall back into fear, but you have received the Spirit of adoption as sons, by whom we cry, "Abba! Father!"
16 – The Spirit himself bears witness with our spirit that we are children of God,

Recognize what is noteworthy and true:

Paul's statement here in verse 14—**"For all who are led by the Spirit of God are sons of God"**—is a continuation of Paul's previous thought. When we reflect on verse 13, we see who receives the power to live by the Spirit. It is the "sons of God" (believers) who are led by the Spirit to do what brings life. Unbelievers might do good things but cannot do what brings life because they are operating in their own strength and flesh, ultimately rejecting God's power and salvation. And one surefire way to know if someone is a son of God is if life-giving fruit is produced consistently throughout that person's lifetime. Notice that this description does not omit female believers. The phrase "sons of God" is just the best way to describe all we, as believers, gain as adopted sons and daughters of God. In ancient times, daughters did not inherit anything unless their husbands inherited something from their families. Therefore, "sons of God" more accurately reflects our position in the Lord. Paul would not have wanted anyone to underestimate all that believers inherit when adopted into the family of God.

In verse 15, Paul urged believers to see what is gained through salvation when he said, **"For you did not receive the spirit of slavery to fall back into fear, but you have received the Spirit of adoption as sons, by whom we cry, 'Abba! Father!'"** Before coming to God for salvation, the spirit of slavery dominated us—creating fear and incessant need to prove ourselves. However, the spirit of slavery can no longer control those who "have received the Spirit of adoption as sons." It can still tempt us but holds no ultimate control over us. Best of all, the heavenly Father loves and cares for His children just like a good earthly father would. The Father's loving relationship with us stands in stark contrast to one where we were dominated and despised by the slave master of sin. Paul highlighted this reality when he combined the Aramaic word "Abba!" with the Greek word "pater" for "Father." "Abba" was an endearing term that Jewish families used, much like we use "daddy" or "papa" today when calling out to our fathers. Paul might have also added the Greek term "pater" here since some in his audience might have been unfamiliar with the Aramaic term "abba." However, doing this also emphasizes the tone and strengthens the tender connection we feel with our Heavenly Father. Because of what Christ did for our redemption, as believers, we can now cry out to God in the most desperate, personal, and tender of ways—"Abba Father!"

Paul then provided even greater assurance of salvation for Christ-followers when he said, **"The Spirit himself bears witness with our spirit that we are children of God,"** (v. 16). In Deuteronomy 17:6, the Jewish law required at least two witnesses to establish a testimony. Thankfully, we have two witnesses to our adoption as children of God—"our spirit" agreeing with the Spirit of God. This also reminds us that the Spirit within the children of God constantly leads believers toward feeling assured and certain of our complete acceptance by God. If you begin to doubt your salvation, you might be falling back into fear—listening to the lies of the spirit of slavery by letting sin and shame lead you astray or, worse still, you might not truly be saved. If either of these are true, you should quickly settle the matter with God, your loving Father, because He welcomes the lost and keeps His covenant with the redeemed.

Thought to take:

This passage benefits not only those who might not be saved but also believers who are insecure in the Father's love and acceptance, which might tempt them to doubt their salvation. Fear and sin must be rejected while trust in Christ must be embraced. Amazingly, this passage also goes further to remind us all of how accessible and intimate the Father's love is for His adopted children, believers in Christ. Having this relationship with the Father assures us we can cry out to and receive from Him His protection and love at all times. We never have to worry that God will abandon or rebuff us when we reach out to Him. If that were not enough, the Spirit also provides believers with the assurance of our salvation by agreeing with our human spirit, confirming our adoption in God's family. Thank the Lord that He does not leave us in the dark about what adoption into His family looks like, is, and can be for those who turn to Christ. As I go about this day, whenever I feel afraid or am giving in to temptation and lies, I will cry out to my Father for His help and deliverance. It is there that I will rest securely in His embrace, rejoicing and knowing He says I am His!

T2t: Feel fear? Turn to the Father!

Help from the Lord: Pray for God's help to apply your T2t both now and all day long.

> *Father, though many people and forces in this life may fail me, reject me, or even disown me, You never will! So why would I ever listen to or be intimidated by the spirit of slavery—returning to sin once again? Why would I run from You, my loving and tender Father, and into the arms of a slave master who only wants to control and dominate me? The choice seems so clear at this moment, but so often I'm deceived and led astray by my human and sinful desires. So as I go about this day, empower me to follow hard after You—to listen to Your Spirit rather than listening to the voice of the spirit of slavery. Use my obedience to following Your lead as a way to deepen my assurance that You are not only with me but living within me. Remind me each day that Your Spirit establishes and declares my adoption into Your family, agreeing with my spirit that I am Yours! Most of all, break down any barriers between us, bringing me to the end of myself so that I rest securely as one of Your own. For I know and believe that with You, there is security and unconditional love! Any fear I feel is just a warning sign that I need to cry out to You, my Abba Father, for peace and assurance once again. Thank You for always being there for me, for always helping me, and for always claiming me as Your own. I love and trust You with my life! In Christ's name, amen.*

Yield to the Lord: Throughout the day, yield your way for God's way, prayerfully reflecting on how you did at the end of your day.

29 – Leaning into Christ's Glory

Week 10, Day 2—Romans 8:17-19

Welcome the Lord!

Open my eyes, that I may behold wondrous things out of your law.
—Psalm 119:18

Observe what the Scripture says:

17 – and if children, then heirs—heirs of God and fellow heirs with Christ, provided we suffer with him in order that we may also be glorified with him.
18 – For I consider that the sufferings of this present time are not worth comparing with the glory that is to be revealed to us.
19 – For the creation waits with eager longing for the revealing of the sons of God.

Recognize what is noteworthy and true:

Paul continued to share the many encouragements the children of God hold (v. 16), saying in verse 17, **"and if children, then heirs—heirs of God and fellow heirs with Christ, provided we suffer with him in order that we may also be glorified with him."** The Greek word used here for "if" can also be translated as "since," indicating Paul was confident that he was talking to people who were children and heirs of God. Paul used the Greek word "kleronomos" for "heir," which depicts both the right to an inheritance from a benefactor and taking hold of the inheritance. If this weren't encouraging enough, Paul also revealed that children of God are coheirs or "fellow heirs with Christ." This inheritance includes both sublime spiritual riches (many we will not discover until eternity) and sorrowful sacrifices—suffering with Christ during our lives on earth. Children of

God must identify with and submit to the sufferings of Christ during our lifetimes, remembering we will also be glorified with Him one day in heaven (1 Peter 1:3-12). Most of us will never be martyrs for our faith, but we will experience rejection and persecution "provided we suffer with him" (Jesus) as we share and live out our faith in a world hostile toward Christ.

In verse 18, Paul lifted this perspective-shifting gem into the light when he said, **"For I consider that the sufferings of this present time are not worth comparing with the glory that is to be revealed to us."** This statement must first be understood in the context of our shared inheritance with Christ—suffering for the sake of the Gospel during the brief time we live on earth. Second, there is absolutely no "comparing" (meaning, calculating) our short time of suffering for Christ here on earth with the glory God will reveal to us as we come face-to-face with Him in heaven. The Greek word Paul used here for "glory" is doxa, meaning to give an accurate, full opinion and estimation of something. On that day in heaven, we will finally be able to take in all of who God is in His character, power, and accomplishments. No wonder it will be such a perspective-shifting sight to behold! Not only will that blow our minds, but all the pain, loss, and tribulation we experienced because of our faith will fade and disappear as God's glory comes into view. All the pain and losses of living in a fallen world will also fade, though this is not the context for what Paul was discussing here. And even though our sufferings now cannot compare with this glorious day in heaven, we must always find encouragement from it, especially when persecuted for our faith.

In verse 19, Paul added, **"For the creation waits with eager longing for the revealing of the sons of God."** Even the creation, in a spiritual sense, longs and leans in with anticipation for the moment God will reveal the sons of God (the redeemed) in heaven. The Greek word Paul used for "revealing" captures the idea of unveiling a masterpiece in all of its perfection and completed beauty. Stop to take that in, friends. Not only are you, as a Christ-follower, a coheir with Christ but you're also His breathtaking masterpiece.

Thought to take:

God has given believers so many blessings. We are not only given the gift of salvation through our faith in Christ but God has also made us heirs with Jesus—the One who made salvation possible in the first place! When we stop to think about all our inheritance brings, it should put into perspective every trial we face, especially when we suffer for Jesus' sake. How often do I stop and think about this when people argue with or reject me for sharing my faith with them? Am I encouraging myself with this current truth and future reality when these conflicts arise? Not nearly as much as I should. So today, I will remind myself that, as a child of God, I must embrace both the hard and the encouraging parts of Jesus' inheritance and calling. Instead of resisting the hard parts, I will see suffering for Christ's sake as a perfect way to bring Him glory now and forever in heaven.

T2t: Suffer for Christ

Help **from the Lord:** Pray for God's help to apply your T2t both now and all day long.

> *Father, thank You for blessing me with both my salvation and my shared inheritance with Christ. I really don't know how Your Son could willingly die for me and then, on top of it all, share His glory and inheritance with me. It's as if I finally think I understand a slice of Your love, only for You to take my understanding to an entirely new and more glorious level. This shows just how bottomless and enduring Your love is for me! So when conflicts emerge because people are offended by what I share about the Gospel, don't let me become discouraged. Instead, lift my eyes and give strength to my heart to see what lies ahead! Help me realize and lean into all that You will reveal one day in heaven because of Your love, grace, and glory. Use that deeper faith and understanding to help me persevere— enduring suffering and injustice because Your Son endured the worst suffering and injustice for my sake. Remind me that it is a great honor to walk where Jesus walked each day. Let this compel me to carry my cross up every hill of adversity—up every hill that leads to dying to my sin and selfishness. I will trust that these choices lead to the abundant life now and will culminate in everlasting life and an amazing inheritance with Christ one day! Your love for me makes accepting all the losses, persecutions, and sufferings of life worth every twinge of pain I might feel! In Jesus' name, amen.*

Yield **to the Lord:** Throughout the day, yield your way for God's way, prayerfully reflecting on how you did at the end of your day.

30 – Worth All the Pain

Week 10, Day 3—Romans 8:20-22

Welcome the Lord!

Open my eyes, that I may behold wondrous things out of your law.
—Psalm 119:18

Observe what the Scripture says:

20 – For the creation was subjected to futility, not willingly, but because of him who subjected it, in hope

21 – that the creation itself will be set free from its bondage to corruption and obtain the freedom of the glory of the children of God.

22 – For we know that the whole creation has been groaning together in the pains of childbirth until now.

Recognize what is noteworthy and true:

As we begin our study today, we must first remember the context—that creation responds with eager anticipation for God to reveal the sons of God (v. 19). But here, we see Paul contrasting that with the negative impact that creation has felt regarding the fall: **"For the creation was subjected to futility, not willingly, but because of him who subjected it, in hope"** (v. 20). The Greek word Paul used for "futility" captures the idea of something that does not measure up to what it was created to do and be. God was the One ("him") who "subjected" (meaning, brought under firm control) an unwilling creation to the curse. Paul's use of the word creation here refers to both humans and the earth. Paul also revealed the far-reaching negative impact of sin, creating a fallen nature in humans and a fallen world when sin entered through Adam. But God did not subject creation to futility without also providing a "hope" we can experience and count on as believers. This hope is not just wishful thinking but an actual future reality, delivering us from death and decay one day while giving us new life today!

In verse 21, Paul explained what this "hope" (v. 20) is, saying, **"that the creation itself will be set free from its bondage to corruption and obtain the freedom of the glory of the children of God."** Although God has subjected creation to futility, He will set creation free one day, releasing it from bondage to corruption (sin) when He reveals the glory of the children of God in heaven. On this glorious and future day, God will remove the full impact of the curse of sin on all creation. The commentaries I researched agree that this is probably speaking of the beginning of Christ's second coming and millennium reign (Jer. 31:12-14; 33). At this future point, creation, particularly "earth," will be transformed but not recreated into a new earth. This transformation will be different than a later event referring to the prophesied "new heaven and a new earth" (Rev. 21:1-2; 2 Pet. 3:11-13). At that time—called the "day of the Lord" (2 Pet. 3:10)—God will destroy both heaven and earth, going on to perfectly recreate both. Regardless of when creation will be set free, we can confidently hope and know that this freedom will happen one glorious day in the future.

In verse 22, Paul painted a picture, suggesting what creation feels as it waits on this glorious day: **"For we know that the whole creation has been groaning together in the pains of childbirth until now."** We also can see and feel what this Scripture describes when we look at what's going on throughout the earth. We are plagued by earthquakes, wars, hurricanes, unrelenting wildfires, pandemics, and the like, giving evidence of the "pains of childbirth." But believers can take heart when we see these signs. Although the pains of childbirth are agonizing, a blessed hope follows the birth of a child. In the same way, our suffering for Christ is worth every bit of pain as we trust in and wait on our Lord's full glory to be revealed.

Thought to take:

It is so easy to become discouraged by all the suffering and mayhem going on all over the world. But that's like watching a woman in the pain of childbirth, not realizing that she is giving birth to a beautiful baby who will bring her tremendous joy. In much the same way, all creation is laboring and in pain, waiting for the glorious day when God will reveal the beautiful children of God in heaven. On that day, not only will God completely free believers from the curse of sin, but He will also set free all of creation from the devastation and bondage our sins have done to all of life. We don't have to wonder if this desired transformation will take place. Through Christ, we can trust that this hope is sure and will come true one day. Because of this, I will cling to and believe in Christ's future hope and reality.

I will also trust that God is taking every pain I feel and see around me, making it worthwhile as I wait for His meaningful and glorious transformation to be born.

T2t: See pain in light of God's hope

Help **from the Lord:** Pray for God's help to apply your T2t both now and all day long.

> *Father, You are so good and loving, taking all that is meaningless and empty and making it meaningful, fruitful, and pure. That's what You are doing and have done with my heart through Your Spirit. And that's also what You will do for all creation one glorious day to come. You never abandon me or other believers to the mess and devastation we make. You are always there redeeming and refining it all here and now but also laboring to bring about a transformed and liberated creation one day. Give me the confidence to trust You in this future reality, hoping with the firm expectation that You will do what You say You will do! And whenever I feel the pain of living on this fallen planet rising higher in my life, turn my heart toward Your hope that I already feel and know today. And whenever I see turmoil, suffering, and devastation happening on this earth, turn my eyes toward the sky, believing You are also laboring in miraculous and glorious ways for all of creation to see and behold one day. Keep my heart trusting and waiting for Your hope! Use this renewed hope as a way to give my life more meaning, strengthening my resolve to trust that You are busy making every ounce of suffering I see and experience worth all the pain. In Christ's name, amen.*

Yield **to the Lord:** The day, yield your way for God's way, prayerfully reflecting on how you did at the end of your day.

Week Ten Questions for Discussion or Contemplation

Read aloud Day 1, Romans 8:14-16 …

1. Share about a time when you felt and knew that God was leading you, and how did you know it was God leading you (v. 14)?

2. What does the encouragement to and privilege of crying out "Abba Father" in prayer tell you about God and your relationship with Him (v. 15)? How do you feel about this right as a child of God?

3. What are the truths or truth principles we might not have talked about yet from verses 14-16 that catch your attention, and why?

Read aloud Day 2, Romans 8:17-19 …

4. What are some of the ways you have seen others suffer for Christ's sake (vv. 17-18)? How have you suffered for Christ's sake?

5. How can we turn any suffering we face into suffering for Christ's sake? What makes it difficult for believers or "you" to do this?

6. What are the truths or truth principles we might not have talked about yet from verses 17-19 that catch your attention, and why?

Read aloud Day 3, Romans 8:20-22 …

7. Knowing creation was subjected to futility, why do you think God didn't just scrap it and start over or abandon it/us altogether (v. 20)?

8. How does viewing our and the world's suffering as "pains of childbirth" change your perspective about this plight (v. 22)?

9. What are the truths or truth principles we might not have talked about yet from verses 20-22 that catch your attention, and why?

10. What is one thing from this past week's study that you want to learn from and live out more?

11. Would anyone like to read a prayer you wrote based on one of the Scriptures from this week? How can we pray for you?

Week Eleven

31 – Wait Patiently

Week 11, Day 1—Romans 8:23-25

Welcome the Lord!

> Open my eyes, that I may behold wondrous things out of your law.
> —Psalm 119:18

Observe what the Scripture says:

23 – And not only the creation, but we ourselves, who have the firstfruits of the Spirit, groan inwardly as we wait eagerly for adoption as sons, the redemption of our bodies.
24 – For in this hope we were saved. Now hope that is seen is not hope. For who hopes for what he sees?
25 – But if we hope for what we do not see, we wait for it with patience.

Recognize what is noteworthy and true:

In verse 23, Paul contrasted what the creation experiences with what the children of God are experiencing: **"And not only the creation, but we ourselves, who have the firstfruits of the Spirit, groan inwardly as we wait eagerly for adoption as sons, the redemption of our bodies."** Those who have the "firstfruits" of the Spirit (the redeemed) inwardly groan just like the creation does. The word Paul used for "have" here was stated in the present tense, emphasizing how we continually possess the firstfruits of the Spirit. And the Greek term he used for "firstfruits" here refers to the first fruit of the Spirit—the Spirit Himself. Even though God adopts those who trust in Christ into His family, there is a more extensive completion (confirmation) of this status occurring when God reveals "the sons of God" (v. 19) and the "redemption of our bodies." Christ will give the sons of God (believers) glorified bodies on that day (Phil. 3:20-21; 1 Cor. 15:44).

In verse 24, Paul added these encouraging truths: **"For in this hope we were saved. Now hope that is seen is not hope. For who hopes for what he sees?"** The process of "adoption as sons" involves a certain level of waiting. Yet our hope, as believers, is secure because, if we trusted Christ as our Savior, "we were saved" (past tense). At various points in chapter 8, Paul taught about our past, current, and future salvation. God saves those who trust Christ immediately and continues saving (sanctifying) believers as we wait on the culmination of our salvation (glorification) in eternity. The Greek word Paul used for "hope" in this verse reflects what we trust is something we already possess through Christ. However, we should not confuse it with "faith in Christ" since God uses our faith as the prompter (not means) for extending His grace and salvation to us. We need the hope of God because we cannot yet see all that God wants to do through our salvation. Our future salvation is something we hope and long for, knowing God will complete it when God reveals the "sons of God" one day (v. 19).

In verse 25, Paul moved from focusing on certain truths about our salvation to what believers must do each day, saying, **"But if we hope for what we do not see, we wait for it with patience."** Our hope in Christ assures us that this day of glorious revealing will truly happen one day. We cannot see into the future to this day, so we hope for and in it. We did not see Christ when He walked the streets of earth, performed miracles, or died on the cross. So we hope now in what Scripture reveals He did and who He is as our Savior. Although good works give evidence of the indwelling Spirit within the redeemed, this does not give us absolute proof. So, we hope—hoping in Christ! The Spirit uses our hope in Christ to strengthen our patience (literally, perseverance) while we wait on God to unfold and complete His plan.

Thought to take:

This passage reminds me that the longer I persevere in my faith, the firmer and more confident my hope is in my salvation in Christ. It's as if God uses the faith that I placed in Christ many years ago to fire up the Spirit's work in me today. The Spirit confirms all along the way in my life my adoption as a child of God, even though there is still more to come! It's somewhat like a little girl who is adopted "on paper" is legally her adoptive parents' child, even though she hasn't come to live with her new family just yet. Still, she confidently looks forward to the grand celebration and future "revealing" of her new, completed family and future home. Ultimately, this gives us, as believers, two choices. We can question or ignore these promises from the Father that prove He adopted us when we placed our faith in Christ. Or we can rest in this current reality and future hope while longing for the day when our complete reunion with our Father occurs. I know which one I will choose! Throughout this day, I will remind myself that I am saved and will continue to wait in the hope of Christ, looking forward to the day when His revealing and completion will come full circle.

T2t: Rest in and look forward with hope

Help from the Lord: Pray for God's help to apply your T2t both now and all day long.

> *Father, I am so grateful Your Spirit works to convince me that You have saved me in the past, continue to save me, and have adopted me as Your child. I haven't always felt that confident. You know how when I was much younger, I often doubted my faith in You. But I doubted it because I couldn't see all that You were doing in my heart and life just yet. Add to that, I didn't understand the importance of the hope-building process that can only develop in the darkness of trials and testing, while learning to wait on You. Thankfully, Your Spirit gives me the ability to grow and trust You more, especially in the things I cannot see, stirring me to find my hope in You alone. Through these choices to be filled with hope, You have deepened my certainty, enabling me to feel confident that I am Your child and always will be part of Your family. I look forward to that homecoming in heaven one day. On that day, my brothers and sisters in Christ and I will revel in Your glory as You reveal us as the sons of God in the glories of heaven. Give me the ability to wait with anticipation, excitement, and perseverance for that precious day to come. Use my hope in You to encourage me every day, especially when troubles and temptations come my way. Use these times to give others a glimpse of Your glory as they see me living out the fruit of Your Spirit in and through Your power alone. In Christ's name, amen.*

Yield to the Lord: Throughout the day, yield your way for God's way, prayerfully reflecting on how you did at the end of your day.

32 – Known, Honed and Blessed

Week 11, Day 2—Romans 8:26-28

Welcome the Lord!

Open my eyes, that I may behold wondrous things out of your law.
—Psalm 119:18

Observe what the Scripture says:

26 – Likewise the Spirit helps us in our weakness. For we do not know what to pray for as we ought, but the Spirit himself intercedes for us with groanings too deep for words.
27 – And he who searches hearts knows what is the mind of the Spirit, because the Spirit intercedes for the saints according to the will of God.
28 – And we know that for those who love God all things work together for good, for those who are called according to his purpose.

Recognize what is noteworthy and true:

In yesterday's reading (vv. 23-25), Paul revealed that the Spirit uses our hope in this glorious future day to help sustain us now. But, here in verse 26, Paul identified yet another way the Spirit works, saying: **"Likewise the Spirit helps us in our weakness. For we do not know what to pray for as we ought, but the Spirit himself intercedes for us with groanings too deep for words."** We live now in what feels like the messy middle of God's redemptive plan and are too weak to even know what to pray without the Spirit's help. So just as both the creation and the sons of God groan, the Spirit groans also, interceding to the Father for our sakes. Thankfully, the Spirit's groanings supersede and go deeper, surpassing our understanding while expressing and addressing our prayer needs more effectively than we can.

In verse 27, Paul then explained how this miraculous prayer process works when he said, **"And he who searches hearts knows what is the mind of the Spirit, because the Spirit intercedes for the saints according to the will of God."** Notice what Paul did and didn't say here. First, when we pray, Paul was quick to say that the Spirit searches our hearts. Something that is both comforting and disconcerting depending on our level of obedience at any given time. But note what Paul didn't say. He didn't say that the Spirit is seeking to know our minds, though the Spirit does know our every thought. What Paul did say is that the Spirit knows "what is in the mind of the Spirit." The Spirit's main purpose for interceding for us is to interpret our feeble prayers and turn them into pleas that conform to God's will, making them pleasing to the Father. We don't have to worry about whether we are praying in the right way or about the right things because the Spirit will not only interpret our prayers correctly but will also use them to bring about a God-honoring response from us. Just think about that for a minute. Our prayers are used by the Spirit to continually conform us to God's will, transforming us each time we pray.

In verse 28, Paul gave us a very encouraging, yet conditional, promise from God when he said, **"And we know that for those who love God all things work together for good, for those who are called according to his purpose."** This promise belongs to "those who love God" and "are called according to his purpose" (believers). This verse also highlights how God enables believers to love Him with sacrificial "agapao" love (God-like love). As believers, we can also "know" and hope confidently that God is working all things together for good—the Lord's perfect good. Not one issue in the believer's life eludes God's good, redemptive purposes as He is always conforming all circumstances to His perfect will. This is a call for all Christ-followers to yield to and live out our calling, pursuing God's purposes rather than our own each day.

Thought to take:

This small passage is packed full of "thoughts" we could "take" with us and apply throughout our day and lives. And the first encouraging thought (truth) I see involves how the Spirit groans and intercedes to the Father for believers through our prayers. This captures such a moving and compassionate response from the Spirit, who feels our distress and knows the seriousness of our situation much more than we do! One "T2t" for today could be to remember how compassionately and intimately the Spirit responds to prayer. The second encouraging thought involves how the Spirit brings the believer's desire in accordance and conformity with God's will. The "T2t" for this could be to know that the Spirit uses prayer to conform me, as a believer, to God's will and desires.

The third even more uplifting thought is that God works all things together for His good when believers continue to pursue His purposes and calling in our lives. A potential "T2t" here could be to trust in God's power, knowing He is taking every trouble and redeeming it into His good for His children. I will focus on all three—the Spirit knows me, hones me to His will, and redeems my troubles.

T2t: I'm known, honed, blessed!

Help from the Lord: Pray for God's help to apply your T2t both now and all day long.

> Father, I'm eternally grateful for Your salvation made available through Your Son. And I enjoy these rights of an adopted son of God as it is the greatest of all gifts and inheritances! But You still bless me more, knowing how weak and feeble my prayers are without Your Spirit interceding and interpreting them for me. This is such a comfort, knowing that Your Spirit cares so deeply about what I care about and ask of You. I'm also relieved, knowing that I don't have to know what to pray or even how to pray because Your Spirit prays through and along with me. But then Your Spirit goes even deeper, conforming me more and more to Your will with every prayer I lift to Your throne. Help me see this transformation taking place in my heart and use it to continually strengthen my devotion to You and Your purposes. Enable me to recognize the wonder, miracle, and blessing of this transformation. As this beautiful reality sinks in, I will praise You for helping me step out in obedience and faith–faith that is fueled by Your Spirit. But that's not where I want my praises to end–not by a long shot! I want to praise and thank You for working everything out for my good, accomplishing Your good and perfect will in my life. You bless me so much more than my words can convey. So I will leave it up to the Spirit, once again, to reflect the deepest yearnings and praises of my heart to You, my Father–the One who cares greatly for me, Your Child! In Christ's name, amen.

Yield to the Lord: Throughout the day, yield your way for God's way, prayerfully reflecting on how you did at the end of your day.

33 – Always For—Never Against

Week 11, Day 3—Romans 8:29-31

Welcome the Lord!

Open my eyes, that I may behold wondrous things out of your law.
—Psalm 119:18

Observe what the Scripture says:

29 – For those whom he foreknew he also predestined to be conformed to the image of his Son, in order that he might be the firstborn among many brothers.
30 – And those whom he predestined he also called, and those whom he called he also justified, and those whom he justified he also glorified.
31 – What then shall we say to these things? If God is for us, who can be against us?

Recognize what is noteworthy and true:

Paul shared an explanation of God's past work in the life of a believer, saying in verse 29: **"For those whom he foreknew he also predestined to be conformed to the image of his Son, in order that he might be the firstborn among many brothers."** The Greek word for "foreknew" is proginosko and involves more than just knowing something will happen in the future. This word describes how God chose and determined ahead of time (predestined) a limited number of people (believers or "elect") to be conformed to Christ (v. 33). This verse also reflects God's constant work of conforming us to Christ's image once we receive salvation. Being conformed to Christ's image is also called sanctification and is the process God uses to help us "work out" our salvation in the day-to-day (Phil. 2:12-13). Jesus is the "firstborn among many brothers" (male and female believers) who are "predestined" to be God's adopted children. In Revelation 1:5 it also says Jesus is athe "firstborn of the dead," which stems from His relationship to creation (Col. 1:15) as Redeemer. Christ is the One who brings new life to those dead in their sins. This term also highlights the superior rank Jesus holds over the children of God. Thankfully, Christ willingly shares His inheritance with all of the children of God (v. 17), offering this to us as our firstborn Brother. The intimate family connections that come from our God continue to expand, giving us comfort and meaning now but also joys that keep on unfolding in eternity.

Paul presented verse 30 like a melodic crescendo that rises higher and higher, as he summarized three ways God sovereignly works in the life of a believer: **"And those whom he predestined he also called, and those whom he called he also justified, and those whom he justified he also glorified."** Paul turned his topic from believers being conformed to the image of the Son (v. 29) to identifying three works God alone does in and for the redeemed. God calls, justifies, and glorifies believers. Before God created the world, He predestined and called certain people to be His own (Eph. 1:4-5). This calling results in the justification (salvation) of believers through our faith in Christ's righteousness. And although the "glorification" of believers has not yet occurred, it is a sure hope and future eventuality (vv. 23-24). We must remember, God alone does the work involved in justification and glorification of believers. However, God expects believers to cooperate with the Spirit to work out—never earn—our salvation in the process of sanctification. (Phil. 2:12).

In verse 31, Paul's melodic message about all that we as children of God receive through His foreordained calling rises still higher with these two inspiring questions: **"What then shall we say to these things? If God is for us, who can be against us?"** If we look back to what Paul had unpacked in the first three chapters of Romans—where God's wrath and judgment come into view—we could feel as if God is against us. Yet when we consider all God has done to redeem, sanctify and, one day, glorify His children, our conclusion could never be He is against us. The only obvious and true conclusion is that God is for us because of all our Father lavishes on His children—then, now, and one day throughout eternity.

Thought to take:

It might be tempting to look at today's reading and only focus on the fact that God chose a select number—the predestined—for adoption into His family. But I, for one, will not question God's merciful and loving plan nor His reasons for choosing those He did (Rom. 9:14-16). Instead, I will focus on the truth that God is, has been, and will always be in perfect control of all of His creation. I will also remind myself that God is never shocked or caught off guard by what is going on in my life, knowing He is using these trials to make me more like Christ. Because of these lavish gifts of love, I will take the opportunity to rejoice, knowing the Father chose me (and, hopefully, you!) before the foundations of the world. I also want to rejoice, recognizing that the One who gave His life for me is my big, sacrificial Brother. As Christ-followers, we are intimately and connected to the Sovereign God of the Universe! When I notice, focus on, and thank God for all the ways He demonstrates His love for me, His child and Christ's sibling, I will grow more and more confident that He is for me no matter what trouble I encounter each day.

T2t: God chose and is for me

Help from the Lord: Pray for God's help to apply your T2t both now and all day long.

> *Father, Your love is so astounding and undeserved, breaking down every barrier to get to me! At one time, I lived my life against You, choosing my own way and doing whatever brought me pleasure. But those pleasures were always short-lived and proved to be utterly meaningless. Thankfully, You knew long before I was born that I could never find hope or meaning in this life outside of Your grace. And, oh what a grace it is! A grace that not only saves me, helps me, but also welcomes me as Your adopted child and part of Your family! Thank You for devising this perfect plan that predestines me and all who trust in Jesus to be Your own. Where would I be if You hadn't called me out of the grave of sin and welcomed me into an intimate relationship with You? Because of this glorious reality, I will praise You all day long for loving and choosing me. I will thank You for giving me a place in Your family, alongside my big Brother—my precious Savoir who loved me with His life! Keep my mind focused on the truth of my salvation today, using it to convince me more and more of Your love. Convince me that no matter what life feels or looks like, You are for me and never against me. I only need to look to You, what You have done for me, are doing now, and will bring about one glorious future day. These are the blessed realities and certainties I will praise You for, knowing You will use them to brighten Your glory now and illuminate all of heaven one day to come. In Christ's name, amen.*

Yield to the Lord: Throughout the day, yield your way for God's way, prayerfully reflecting on how you did at the end of your day.

Week Eleven Questions for Discussion or Contemplation

Read aloud Day 1, Romans 8:23-25 ...

1. What are some ways you "groan inwardly" for your adoption as God's child and redemption of your body (v. 23)?

2. What are some specific things we can do to grow more patient, persevering in the hope of Christ (v. 25)?

3. What are the truths or truth principles we might not have talked about yet from verses 23-25 that catch your attention, and why?

Read aloud Day 2, Romans 8:26-28 ...

4. What are some issues you have difficulty praying for in your life, and why is it difficult (v. 26)? Describe what you think the Spirit is doing and achieving when He helps you in your weakness?

5. What situation in your life do you sometimes doubt God will work together for good, and what causes doubt (v. 28)? What does verse 28 promise and *not* promise?

6. What are the truths or truth principles we might not have talked about yet from verses 26-28 that catch your attention, and why?

Read aloud Day 3, Romans 8:29-31 ...

7. What do you think predestination means? What gives Jesus the right to predestine or elect certain people to be His own (vv. 29-30)?

8. What statements or truths in verses 29-31 assure believers that "God is for us"? How much are you trusting this is the truth?

9. What are the truths or truth principles we might not have talked about yet from verses 29-31 that catch your attention, and why?

10. What is one thing from this past week's study that you want to learn from and live out more?

11. Would anyone like to read a prayer you wrote based on one of the Scriptures from this week? How can we pray for you?

Week Twelve

34 – Christ Rests His Case

Week 12, Day 1—Romans 8:32-34

Welcome the Lord!

Open my eyes, that I may behold wondrous things out of your law.
—Psalm 119:18

Observe what the Scripture says:

32 – He who did not spare his own Son but gave him up for us all, how will he not also with him graciously give us all things?
33 – Who shall bring any charge against God's elect? It is God who justifies.
34 – Who is to condemn? Christ Jesus is the one who died—more than that, who was raised—who is at the right hand of God, who indeed is interceding for us.

Recognize what is noteworthy and true:

Paul continued his truthful and persuasive argument here, reminding us of what predestined (believers) receive through Christ: **"He who did not spare his own Son but gave him up for us all, how will he not also with him graciously give us all things?"** (v. 32). The Greek word Paul used here for "spare" is "pheidomai." In Hebrew this same word was used but was translated as "withhold" in Genesis 22:12 and 16, when Abraham did not withhold his son from God but willingly offered him as a sacrifice. The word association between these two events reminds us of how Abraham's willingness to sacrifice his son foreshadows the Father's sacrifice of His own Son. Abraham's sacrifice does not compare to the depth of the Father's, though it subtly and selflessly reflects it. The fact that the Father gave up His Son "for us all" proves just how graciously sacrificial He is. Paul's use of the word "graciously" here also reminds us that these "things" are gifts and not things we can earn or deserve. God gives His best and most precious gifts out of His grace, starting from the most precious of these—Christ—letting grace flow downward with abundance, power, and forgiveness from our loving Savior's side.

In verse 33a, Paul asked another perspective-shifting question, **"Who shall bring any charge against God's elect?"** He then gave the undeniable answer in verse 33b, declaring, **"It is God who justifies."** If the Son served as the perfect and complete sacrifice for our sins—*and He did*—what charge could anyone bring against God's elect? Who could call them guilty and unjustified? It's almost as if Paul was describing a courtroom scene. On one side is God, our just Judge. On the other side stands our prosecutor, Satan, accusing us of all the sins we've ever committed and even some we have not (Rev. 12:10). But our Judge throws the accuser's—really, any believer's—charges out because Christ already paid the penalty for the sins of those He redeemed. We are declared innocent—case closed.

In verse 34a, Paul drove his point home with this question, **"Who is to condemn?"** Then, once more, Paul reminded us of this indisputable truth in verse 34b, **"Christ Jesus is the one who died—more than that, who was raised—who is at the right hand of God, who indeed is interceding for us."** Paul's question—"who condemns?"—is a subtle reference to Romans 8:1. The truth is: "There is therefore now no condemnation for those who are in Christ Jesus" (8:1). As believers, there are many who might try to condemn us, including ourselves. But we now have a perfect and powerful Advocate who "intercedes for us." Again, if this were a courtroom scene, we would see Christ standing up to represent and defend believers before the Judge, God the Father. Because Jesus fully paid the penalty for our sin, He can and does graciously extend His nail-scarred hand to the elect, removing the guilt from our sin-stained hands. Since God raised Christ from the dead, He also provides the elect with new life whenever we believe and place our faith in Jesus alone to save us (Jn. 11:25).

Thought to take:

The love the Father has for us is so great that He not only willingly gave His Son for our sakes but also graciously gives us all things (2 Pet. 1:3). But that's only one side of our redemption story. Jesus loves us so much that He died and now intercedes before the Father for us. Now, no one can bring a charge that strips the redeemed of their God-given salvation. No "condemning" accusation can ever be deemed valid when Christ's righteousness covers our hearts. I don't know about you, but it's so easy for me to feel the weight of condemnation and shame, especially when I continue to sin. But we can resist carrying this weight if we remember that Christ defends believers, and the Father declares us not guilty through the sacrifice of His Son's life. We still must regularly get our hearts right with God, repenting when we sin. But our sins do not cancel or take away the enduring "positional forgiveness"* God gives us at salvation. The Father never takes His saving forgiveness away from anyone who trusts in Christ. I want to recognize and meditate on these gifts from God throughout my day. I know these gifts and realities will help me combat my inner critic. They also will invalidate the claims of anyone who questions my faith in Jesus. Most of all, they will help me resist the condemnation of the accuser (Satan) when he attacks my mind. I will rest in Christ's defense, knowing this will keep me encouraged in my faith and empowered in my life.

T2t: Rest in Christ's defense

Help from the Lord: Pray for God's help to apply your T2t both now and all day long.

> Father, I am so moved by the thought of Jesus being the Advocate who defends me before You and any accusers. I truly am guilty of the crimes the evil one brings against me. Yet Jesus stands ready to defend me–the defenseless and indefensible–by His grace and redemption! Keep me from ever feeling like I can stand before You and defend my actions when my sins sent Jesus to the cross. And open my eyes to the times I arrogantly try to reason with You, pointing out how my good outweighs my bad, appealing to Your justice rather than Your mercy. When and if I make these defenses, I'm sure the accuser sits back and laughs at me, saying "See, Judge! That fool is as guilty as the day is long!" But, suddenly, silence falls over the courtroom as Jesus stands before You, covering my guilt with His blood and perfect sacrifice. No longer is there a need to prosecute me because Christ took the punishment I deserved so You can declare me" not guilty" and set me free! Use my increasing awareness and gratitude about Christ's sacrifice to move me toward greater devotion to You. Enable me to rest more securely in Your grace, never listening to anyone condemning or accusing me of sins You have forgiven through Your Son. Instead, keep me walking out of that courtroom and into the freedom and provision You shower on me daily. And I will bless You all of my days for blessing me so richly through Christ. In Jesus' name, amen.

Yield to the Lord: Throughout the day, yield your way for God's way, prayerfully reflecting on how you did at the end of your day.

* https://www.gotquestions.org/confession-forgiveness.html

35 – God's Love Conquers All

Week 12, Day 2—Romans 8:35-37

Welcome the Lord!

Open my eyes, that I may behold wondrous things out of your law.
—Psalm 119:18

Observe what the Scripture says:

35 – Who shall separate us from the love of Christ? Shall tribulation, or distress, or persecution, or famine, or nakedness, or danger, or sword?
36 – As it is written, "For your sake we are being killed all the day long; we are regarded as sheep to be slaughtered."
37 – No, in all these things we are more than conquerors through him who loved us.

Recognize what is noteworthy and true:

In yesterday's Scripture passage, Paul identified three gifts that believers receive from God (vv. 32-34). These gifts of "all things" (v. 32) flow from the grace of God. The first gift involves the freedom God gives us—through Christ's salvation—from the penalty of sin (damnation to hell). The second gift is God's intercession for us through the Spirit. The third gift frees us from condemnation since our Savior redeems us from the guilt of our sins.

With these gifts as the backdrop, Paul went on in verse 35 to assert beautiful truths cloaked as questions: **"Who shall separate us from the love of Christ? Shall tribulation, or distress, or persecution, or famine, or nakedness, or danger, or sword?** God's graciousness not only gives evidence of His love for us but also proves that nothing can come between or *separate* us from Christ's love.

The Greek word Paul used for "tribulation" here is "thlipsis" and describes extreme, crushing hardships in life. We all experience suffering in life, but the context for these tribulations involves being persecuted for our faith. The Greek word Paul used for "distress" captures the idea of a person being blocked in with no way of escape. Christ is present in these confined spaces where doom presses in, loving and comforting not only those who suffer for Him but also those who face death for His sake. "Famine" here likely represents persecution involving physical starvation, spiritual hunger, or both. If we are imprisoned or left destitute because of our faith, we might also experience "nakedness" during times like these. The words "danger" and "sword" remind us that our lives might be threatened or taken because of our faith. Yet we can rest assured that in all of these dark and dire situations, nothing can separate us from the love of Christ.

In verse 36, Paul quoted Psalm 44:22, **"For your sake we are being killed all the day long; we are regarded as sheep to be slaughtered."** True believers are often referred to in Scripture and sometimes directly by Christ as sheep since He is our Shepherd. Part of the significance of this has to do with the Jewish sacrifice of a lamb as an offering to God. Another part illustrates how much sheep need their shepherd since they are prone to wander and fall into peril. Just as Christ was led to the cross and slaughtered, when we follow our Shepherd's lead, we face the possibility of death for His sake too. Christ's calling to believers always includes the potential of persecution, tribulation, and death for His sake—death in a variety of ways. It is death to all we desire so that His desires reign supreme.

Paul moved toward his conclusion with this stirring rallying cry, **"No, in all these things we are more than conquerors through him who loved us"** (v. 37). When we face trials and conflicts, we feel tempted to draw the same conclusion as the world, thinking these troubles are to be dreaded and avoided. But as believers, we must see them differently—with Christ always in view. Being "more than conquerors" describes the power Christ gives us to surpass ordinary victories, defeating every enemy or trouble that comes our way. Think of it this way ... Christ gives believers the same amount of power and love that He wielded when He conquered death, sin, and the grave. Nothing could be greater and no victory sweeter.

Thought to take:

As followers of Christ, we must know and embrace two crucial aspects of our calling. First, we will suffer for our faith. We might not face persecution to the point of death but we all will face opposition and trials to varying degrees because of our faith in Christ. Second, the loving presence and power of Christ will always be right there with believers in our times of suffering, making us more than conquerors in all these things. Jesus is always with us when we face persecution for our faith. But He is also with us—loving and comforting us—in every sorrow stemming from living in this broken and fallen world. I want to embrace this truth about my loving Savior, moving it more deeply into my heart with each passing day. If I do, whenever I'm tempted to think I am all alone and up against the world, His loving presence will remind me He is with me. I'll also remember He gives me His same resurrection power, assuring me the victory in every trial. As troubles come my way today, and especially when those troubles are because of my faith in Christ, I will rely on and apply these truths. I will know that Christ is always with me, loving and empowering me to be more than a conqueror in all these things.

T2t: More than a conqueror through Christ!

Help from the Lord: Pray for God's help to apply your T2t both now and all day long.

> *Father, I can easily lose sight of the harsh side of this reality and calling, while ignoring the blessed side of it too. You know how often I view my difficult circumstances as problems rather than as opportunities for my faith to grow deeper. When I do this, I fail to notice and feel Your loving presence moving more powerfully toward me. So instead of doubting You, help me take any ungrateful or negative thoughts captive, replacing these with what I know is true about You and worthy of Your praise. Because, paradoxically, there is so much to praise You for in every trouble and trial! So whenever You call me to suffer for Your sake, heighten my awareness of Your love and loving presence as You move closer toward me. Keep me from fighting these battles in my own strength, knowing I never fight alone. You are always with me, using each distress and struggle as a way to strengthen my faith in You, Your love, and Your conquering power. Empower me to seize the opportunities to live for You, sharing the gospel because I know You have already made me a conqueror in all these things and so much more. Don't ever let me keep Your love and overcoming power all to myself. Instead, make it my mission to freely and confidently share it with all who will listen and learn about Your Son, the One who is my loving and mighty Savior. In Christ's name, amen.*

Yield to the Lord: Throughout the day, yield your way for God's way, prayerfully reflecting on how you did at the end of your day.

36 – Sure of His Love

Week 12, Day 3—Romans 8:38-39

Welcome the Lord!

Open my eyes, that I may behold wondrous things out of your law.
—Psalm 119:18

Observe what the Scripture says:

38 – For I am sure that neither death nor life, nor angels nor rulers, nor things present nor things to come, nor powers,
39 – nor height nor depth, nor anything else in all creation, will be able to separate us from the love of God in Christ Jesus our Lord.

Recognize what is noteworthy and true:

Paul comes to a close in this chapter, saying, **"For I am sure that neither death nor life,"** (v. 38), offering the first contrast between several words and ideas. Even though this verse is only part of a phrase, it provides an all-encompassing reminder of our Savior's constant presence and grace-fueled help. And Paul was sure of this truth because he had lived and experienced it in every possible way—except through death—which would come soon enough for him. Paul used the Greek word "peitho" in this verse for the word "sure"—meaning persuaded or convinced. Since Paul wrote this word in the perfect tense, it alludes to a past event that continually progresses. Paul became sure in the past then continued to grow more convinced of the truth of Christ's love as he saw the Spirit in action throughout his life. It is important to note how Paul mentioned "death" here first, following it up with "life." He likely said it this way, giving it prominence because we fear death more than anything else in life. However, for believers, the very thing we might dread—death—is also the gateway to spending eternity with our loving Savior. Ironically, death results in the best outcome of all believers! Amazingly, even the worst circumstance in life—death—cannot separate Christ-followers from Christ.

Paul went on to list five more threats we face in life: **"nor angels nor rulers, nor things present nor things to come, nor powers,"** (v. 38). The mention of "angels" here probably refers to fallen angels or demons, reminding us not to fear nor worship these beings as some people foolishly did in Paul's day. With the term, "rulers," Paul was most likely alluding to demonic rulers in the spiritual realm rather than earthly rulers. However, when Paul spoke of "powers," he might have had earthly rulers in mind. Paul knew how our fear of any troubles happening now or challenges in the future could distract, discourage, and defeat us. So he wanted us to rest in and rely on the help, strength, and victory of our Conqueror "in all these things" (v. 37).

In verse 39, Paul's lengthy list concluded with these rousing words, **"nor height nor depth, nor anything else in all creation, will be able to separate us from the love of God in Christ Jesus our Lord."** The word "height" here might allude to a high spiritual wall, barrier, or fortress that keeps us from accessing God (2 Cor. 10:5). But it's more likely that Paul was pointing to the heights and vastness of the spiritual realm, where spiritual forces of evil currently attack us, since he also linked it to "depths" (the depths of hell). As believers, we battle in a spiritual warzone daily (Eph. 6:10-20), but we will never be beyond Christ's reach, love, and conquering power. Additionally, believers will never be banished to the depths of hell nor separated from the love of God at any point. The power of Christ's love and grace hold the redeemed steady and secure in all these things. Though we may feel threatened in this life, we must remember that no person, predicament, or power can separate us from our Savior's love nor stop His certain victory in our lives.

Thought to take:

Paul could be so sure about these truths because his faith had been tested—except by death—in every kind of trial. Some five to seven years later, Paul was executed, most likely by a gruesome Roman beheading for his faith, offering the final test of his faith. A test he passed with flying colors! With each form of persecution and conflict Paul went through as a believer, he always kept his focus on the inseparability of Christ and the Lord's triumphant love. This confident trust gave Paul the victory over the temptation to fear, doubt, complain, grow bitter, or lose hope. Each painful loss, trial, and injustice convinced him more and more that Christ was always with him. I will do the same today, focusing on this promise and truth—Christ and His love are always with me! He is always with you and me in every good and bad time in our lives. Paradoxically, His loving power and presence can be felt, seen, and experienced all the more powerfully when we suffer for His sake. So every time I'm persecuted for my faith, I will trust God, allowing my trials to deepen my confidence in Christ's love.

T2t: Let trials deepen my faith

Help from the Lord: Pray for God's help to apply your T2t both now and all day long.

> *Father, this reading reminds me of just how paradoxical Your ways and plan are for my life. You use the very things that cause me to dread as a way to deepen my confidence in You and Your love. Ironically, these restrictive, painful, and fearful places and situations are where I can vividly see Your love coming to my rescue. I see You better in those times than when everything in life is easy and smooth. Thank You for growing my faith in Your love during these painful moments. As I reflect on the hardships in my life, I can see how You have used every single one to deepen our bond. You move closer, making Your grace and love feel more real to me when I suffer than when I am free of pain. I see You using difficulties and tests to prove that You are with me in every crisis and trial—a much-needed confidence booster. So whenever I'm mistreated or suffer for Your sake, unleash Your love in my heart and life, helping me with Your powerful grace to persevere. Enable everyone to see, including me, Your grace and love holding me above the fray and dismay of life. And I will focus on how much You love me, knowing You use each hardship as a divine catalyst for deepening and strengthening my faith in You. In Christ's name, amen.*

Yield to the Lord: Throughout the day, yield your way for God's way, prayerfully reflecting on how you did at the end of your day.

Week Twelve Questions for Discussion or Contemplation

Read aloud Day 1, Romans 8:32-34 ...

1. Let's brainstorm! What are "all things" God graciously gives believers (vv. 32-34)?

2. What do you think the advocacy of Christ means and includes for believers (vv. 33-34)? What does His intercession for believers mean and include (vv. 33-34)?

3. What are the truths or truth principles we might not have talked about yet from verses 32-34 that catch your attention, and why?

Read aloud Day 2, Romans 8:35-37 ...

4. Describe a situation you've faced in the past that tempted you to think you were all alone (v. 35). How can we better integrate the truth that we are never separated from Christ into our lives in moments of doubt and fear?

5. What do you think "more than a conqueror" includes and perhaps doesn't include? How can knowing you are "more than a conqueror" through Christ shift your perspective when you suffer (v. 37)?

6. What are the truths or truth principles we might not have talked about yet from verses 35-37 that catch your attention, and why?

Read aloud Day 3, Romans 8:38-39 ...

7. What are some of the things in this life (mentioned in verses 38-39) that cause you anxiety and test your faith? What gets in the way of or hinders your faith?

8. What are some things we can do to grow as sure and confident as Paul of the constancy of Christ's love (v. 39)?

9. What are the truths or truth principles we might not have talked about yet from verses 38-39 that catch your attention, and why?

10. What is one thing from this past week's study that you want to learn from and live out more?

11. Would anyone like to read a prayer you wrote based on one of the Scriptures from this week? How can we pray for you?

Made in the USA
Columbia, SC
19 March 2023

14011791R00100